What the RICH Do!

What They Have and How They Keep It

(The Financial and Investment Habits
of Canada's Most Successful People)

D0981130

1997

2nd Edition

What the RICH Do!

What They Have and How They Keep It

(The Financial and Investment Habits
of Canada's Most Successful People)

Jerry White

Warwick Publishing
Toronto Los Angeles

© 1997 Jerry White

ISBN 1-895629-88-8
Published by Warwick Publishing Inc.
24 Mercer Street
Toronto, ON.
M5V 1H3

Design: Kimberley Davison
Editorial Services: Harry Endrulat

Printed and bound in Canada by Tri-Graphic Printing (Ottawa) Ltd.

To the Canadian middle class. The best people on earth from the best country on earth; the land where the streets are paved with gold.

Contents

Preface

to the 2nd Edition, 1997

When we launched *What the Rich Do* in 1996, we
had no idea how successful it would be. Our goal was
simply to observe the behaviour of Canada's top 1% of
income earners and to find what they did in terms of
their financial behaviour that was perhaps unique or
different, consistent with other successful people and
potentially different from the middle class.

The idea was to see if we could find some universal
behaviour and core strategies that enhanced success.
It has often been said that to succeed in life one of the
best strategies is to find successful people, identify
their strategy, then replicate it for yourself.

If we observe the strategies of the great money man-
agers and investors such as Professor Benjamin
Graham of Columbia University, Warren Buffet, Sir
John Templeton, George Soros, Philip Fisher, and
Peter Lynch, we can learn valuable lessons, strategies,
and role models to follow.

The same approach applies to the most financially
successful in Canada. We learned that they own equities, invest for the long term, seek knowledge, use a
multi-part plan that is synergistically interrelated (we
called it the Group of Seven), tend to financial advisors, and believe in Canada.

The middle class can learn many things that can
improve their financial performances by replicating
the elements to be found in this book. It is built on

success and research and is uniquely Canadian in approach and situation.

During the period from the research to the launch of the national TV series with TVOntario, Access Alberta, The Knowledge Network, and The Saskatchewan Educational Authority to date, we have conducted over 300 seminars presenting the ideas and strategies of *What the Rich Do.*

We have received valuable feedback and added to the research with new ideas and concepts to build on what we have. The series will continue for many years, and we hope the sequel, *Your Family's Money*, will be as well received.

In this new edition of the book, we have built on core ideas, enhanced concepts and created principles. We hope it is more complete, easier to follow, and of even greater interest and benefit as a core strategy book for the Canadian investor.

Jerry White
April 1997

Foreword

When we first undertook this study of Canada's top 1% of income earners and asset holders, it was to determine if they had or did something unique that contributed to their financial success. As Canadian companies do little or no research, relying instead on U.S. or British data, it was an interesting challenge getting this research funded.

Canada is a unique and distinct market. Our systems for investing are different from other countries, as are our laws, institutions, and tax structures. And, of course, our culture makes us very different.

Financially, we tend to be more cautious. We are fixated on fixed income securities and real estate, partially out of the long standing Calvinist tradition of thrift and conservatism and partially because of the bank dominance of our financial markets which gives us far less choice than our American neighbours.

We felt in undertaking this research in English and French in all ten provinces that we could learn valuable and revealing lessons that would be of benefit to all Canadians. Perhaps, if the rich were more successful as investors then there may be common reasons that could be applied to all Canadians regardless of their age, income, education, or marital status.

Perhaps, if more people invested and did financial planning as the rich do, they could save more, earn, keep more, pay less tax, and have greater financial security.

While we cannot guarantee financial security or wealth, I think we did find certain strategies such as the "Group of Seven" that not only work but come as close to a science of personal finance as anything made available to Canadians today.

This is not a collection of meaningless clichés such as "save 10%." Our research shows men need to have 15% and women 18-23% of net income to approach any meaningful level of financial security. Everything in this book is researched and fact-based.

We do not present tax minutia or piecemeal approaches. We do not tell you to take your money and run. Rather, we focus on the true pragmatics for Canadians. What really works and what doesn't? What will reduce your risk, preserve your capital, and enhance your returns? Facts not fiction.

To do this research, we needed the support of many people who could share this vision of education and understanding. Our first supporter was Dun & Bradstreet Canada Research, with Zeev Landesberg, vice president of marketing, and Dave Lyons, director of research. They implemented our field research questionnaires, selected the sample, conducted the interviews, and tabulated the results. Without this support, there would be no data.

We then went to Canada's foremost oil and gas investment company, NCE Resources, for support in presenting this to the personal finance community. John Driscoll, president, did not have to take the risk of moving from a general awareness strategy to an educational approach, but he did.

Great change only comes from people of courage and character who believe in the importance of vision and of sharing it with others. Many people did not respond well to this research. It was too pragmatic. It deviated from vague generalities and previous misconceptions. It challenged conventional wisdom. It was factual and criticized traditional institutions. It could liberate the public from a dependency on government. It could work!

Once again, others rose up to the challenge of courage, risk-taking, and innovation. AGF Mutual Funds, led by Warren Goldring, Blake Goldring, and Eric Grove, gave us blanket, unquestioned support to bring the concepts of *WHAT THE RICH DO* to television. With their support (with no strings attached), we worked to produce the series, book, and software to aid and educate the Canadian public. TVOntario assisted us in crafting the series and clearing the network in British Columbia, Alberta, and Saskatchewan. Our producers at Re:Source Media Inc., Mel Goldberg and Kevin Fox, have done a masterful job in bringing this concept to a visual reality.

Laurent Hasson designed our software, and Robert Walker, my longtime business partner, helped to craft this book. Numerous others, too many to mention, have contributed endless hours making this idea of financial independence through knowledge and facts a powerful reality.

WHAT THE RICH DO: What They Have & How They Keep It is just one step on a road of constant research.

Our focus is on chasing success and personal responsibility on doing the right things for yourself and your future in the greatest country on earth — Canada.

Jerry White

"The Greatest Enemy of Good is Better."
— Voltaire

Introduction

A PRACTICAL GUIDE FOR EVERY CANADIAN

This is a book about success. It is about learning from those who have succeeded in building long-term financial security. It is not about greed, or making money for its own sake, or tiny tax tips, or an Armageddonist's view of Canada's economy. It is a positive, action-oriented, knowledge-based perspective about what actually works. It is based on Canadians, by Canadians, and for Canadians.

My view of the world is that I am always thankful for being a Canadian. Even the U.N. over the last three years has rated Canada as number one in the world in terms of quality of life. Despite this, Canadians seem to revel in hearing negative ideas and thoughts about this country. They keep waiting for a collapse that never comes. They want to be told bad things: "take your money and get out," "the government will destroy you," "this country is falling apart and everything we know and believe in is wrong or bad for you." I have always refused to stoop to this level of meaningless drivel.

Canada's financial environment is what it is. We must develop long-term effective strategies to cope with it and succeed, despite various adversities. We must gain knowledge and act upon it, rather than be paralyzed by fear, negative ideas, and inaction.

Yes, the dollar is on par with Club Z points. The economy is burdened with too much government regulation. Taxes have increased 1,167% since 1961. Personal savings have dropped nearly 20% in five years. Net family disposable income is where it was in 1984. The average age for retirement for males is sixty-one. The Canada Pension Plan has an unfunded liability of $580 billion. Only ten insurance companies have Standard and Poor's credit ratings greater than Confederation Life had when it went under. Average investment returns have dropped 3% because of the decline in net fixed income security rates. Eighty-two percent of women over sixty-five live partially or totally on government assistance. The government has targeted those over sixty-five for their new tax assault with clawbacks and withholding taxes. Real estate has dropped to the lowest return vehicle of the 1990s and because of demographics will not resurrect until after 2010.

Things have changed.

Real leadership, financial or otherwise, comes from developing strategies for dealing with change successfully in the long term. All the conventional wisdom of the '60s, '70s, and '80s lacks validity in 1997. Things are different, and compound interest, real estate, and governments must play dramatically wiser roles in our financial futures. Inflation is a nonissue, and taxes rise each year because credits and deductions are no longer indexed as long as inflation is under 3%. Job security for the middle aged and the middle class is a thing of the past. Twenty percent of the total middle-aged, middle management workforce has been downsized, outplaced, and terminated, including over 100,000 government jobs. Society has changed, as have our roles and what we must do.

As a people, we are living longer, earning less, saving less, and yet we need more if we wish to have financial piece of mind. Canadians need growth in their investments at least until age seventy-five not sixty-five — ten years longer than most of us have planned. Women, in particular, need greater returns. Traditionally women live longer, earn 72.5% of what men do, save less as a result, and need more. Women need to not only save more, but they need returns on average 6% higher than men.

Yet women tend to be vertical investors, owning savings bonds and GICs and leaving their money in dormant bank accounts earning minimal interest. This is a national tragedy. Women who are single parents are most likely to be living in poverty. Only 1% of women will retire wealthy, only 6% will retire financially secure, and 14% must work after age sixty-five in order to live an adequate lifestyle.

Rather than taking a passive victim approach to these changes in our society, we chose to undertake a national research study to actually determine how the "rich respond" in this environment. Perhaps we learn more from those who seem to have the best coping strategy than we can from those who either complain or choose to do nothing.

In the fall of 1994, we commenced the design of the study. We identified that Canada's top 1% consist of about 280,000 individuals who earned at least $150,000 a year or more and had a net worth excluding their principal residence of greater than $500,000. This had to be active income actually earned and assets not inherited.

We identified a sample in each of the ten provinces and designed the questionnaire in both official languages, including men and women over twenty-five and under seventy-nine.

We conducted the interviews over a two-month period and completed a national representative sample that was accurate to within 1%.

What we found were some amazing commonalties of behaviour. If a national sample of successful people reveals they do very similar things to ensure this success, then there are lessons here for everyone that could make a difference in the long term.

The Group of Seven

(It's not the McMichael Collection)

WHAT IS A CANADIAN?

A Canadian is someone who eats Chinese food, drives a German car, wears Italian clothes and French perfume, watches American movies on a Japanese TV, and still thinks free trade is not a good idea for Canada.

Because this is a study of success, I thought it imperative that we learn from people who have achieved it through experience, education, and advice. The rich are different, but they offer us all valuable lessons about investment and financial-planning practice.

For example, the rich are acquisitors, investors, and wealth builders. It is the core of their total existence. Achievement is critical, and the building of net worth, assembling wealth long term, and investing are major parts of their lives. The orientation is not towards greed but towards making the wealth creation process a daily function.

The rich are better educated than the general population: 59% have either a university degree or postgraduate education. They are also entrepreneurial and many are heads of their own companies. Eighty-six percent are between thirty-five and sixty-four years of age. Ninety-eight percent own their own homes, not as an investment but as a lifestyle choice.

They are heavy information seekers: 70% use information other than an advisor such as newsletters, research reports, radio, TV, and magazines for financial information. Rich women tend to read more than men and seek out more media such as TV before making any investment decisions. These women are better educated, entrepreneurial, and between thirty-five and fifty-four years of age. They are more computer literate than men and tend to use financial planning software.

These rich Canadians are self-directed, independent, and informed. They consult spouses on investment decisions. They are positive, assertive, action-oriented people who are not afraid of market declines or short-term market psychology.

They have estate plans, retirement plans, wills, powers of attorney, maximum RRSP investments, life insurance to protect their families, and essentially all the things you would expect of people who live "by the book" of financial achievement. They do what they are supposed to do when they are supposed to do it.

Although most are long-term buy-and-hold investors, they update and review their financial plans more than once a year.

Sixty-five percent invest internationally, not because they fear their future in Canada but because they understand it is essential to reduce risk and build better returns. About a third leverage (borrow) to invest in order to get greater returns.

Seventy-three percent of rich men and 83% of rich women have a personal computer and use it for their financial planning and asset management. They understand the power of the technology and its benefits if used properly.

Sixty percent subscribe to financial newsletters, the internet, financial magazines, and newspapers.

CANADA'S NEW "GROUP OF SEVEN"

At no time in our financial history has there been a greater need for personal financial planning because of an aging population, benefit clawbacks, withholding taxes, and a mountain of national debt.

Everyone needs to establish a seven-component plan that redefines our long-term financial security. The new Group of Seven — the seven pillars of financial security — are a fact of life in the 1990s.

1. A Personal Financial Plan

Where does my money come from, where does it go, and why? How can I maximize my return and minimize wasteful impulse buying and nondeductible costs? How can I build long-term security?

2. An Investment Plan

How can I preserve capital, reduce my risk, and enhance the returns of all the assets I own at the lowest possible tax cost? What is my risk orientation? What is the optional allocation of my holdings between equities, bonds, cash, real estate, and tangible property? What level of diversification do I need to maximize profit and reduce the risk to my capital?

3. A Tax Plan

Why do I pay as much tax as I do? Are there better investments and strategies to reduce this tax? Can I reduce my withholding tax and enhance my cash flow? What are the lowest risk tax ameliorated investments, and can I borrow to finance them? How can I eliminate nondeductible interest expense? How can I reduce the tax on my retirement and estate?

4. A Retirement Plan

How can I assure a comfortable and secure retirement without undertaking too much investment risk? How can I assure the comfortable retirement of my spouse and reduce our taxes? What level of savings, investments, and diversification is needed to achieve this goal? What holdings do I need beyond the RRSP, CPP, OAS, and company pension plan?

5. An Estate Plan

How can I preserve my capital and insure it passes safely to my beneficiaries at the lowest tax cost? How do I avoid provincial probate fees and federal deemed disposition taxes on my death? What assets should I sell or hold jointly with my spouse? What level of insurance is needed to insure I will provide properly for all contingencies?

6. A Will

Who should be the beneficiaries and how can family assets be preserved? How often should it be updated and what other factors should I provide for such as the family business, cottage, collectibles, and charity?

7. A Power of Attorney for Financial and Personal Care

How can I insure that if I am ever incapacitated my assets will be protected, my wishes will be carried out, and the right party, such as my spouse or children, will be empowered to act for me?

We do not need a few of these, we need all seven. Do them all or risk losing it all. This is the new financial absolute of the 1990s.

ARE YOU DIFFERENT?

Do you feel different? You should, because you are. In a North American culture and economy dominated by American capital, financial institutions, media and general business, political and social hyperactivity, too often the unique persona associated with being a Canadian is either misunderstood or, worse, ignored. To anyone who bothers to look closely, Canadians are much more than first cousins within an extended American family. This reality is also reflected in our different financial priorities, spending habits, and investment opportunities. Canadian investors are unique financial creatures. All too often our own professional advisors overlook this fact.

Recently, I had the honour of being asked to be the opening speaker at a major financial services industry conference at the Royal York Hotel in Toronto sponsored by the Institute for International Research. In preparing for this presentation, it struck me that this event would be an appropriate forum to remind my colleagues in the financial industry (some of whom may be your financial advisors) of this fact.

But, on further reflection I thought to myself, why save my comments on this important subject for a select group of industry insiders only? After all, isn't it really individual Canadian investors who count most?

But, if Canadians are financially different from Americans, how so? First of all, Canadians live in a unique economic environment which has produced a more conservative investment psychology. For example, Canadians:

- are confronted with much higher personal tax rates than Americans, yet historically have saved money at a rate almost twice that of Americans (although the gap is narrowing);

- live longer than Americans on average (by about 5%);

- are, on average, better educated with better access and exposure to media;

- have better retirement savings vehicles but fewer investment options.

Ask any foreigner and nine times out of ten you will find a clear perception of differences between Canadians and Americans. Two recent international studies give us important clues about how we are perceived by the rest of the world.

The first study was a 1995 World Bank report in which Canada was recognized as the second wealthiest country in the world (slightly behind Australia) on a per capita basis. It calculated that each Canadian was "worth" U.S.$704,000. In contrast, each U.S. citizen was worth only U.S.$421,000 (which placed the United States twelfth overall).

The World's Wealthiest Countries

Country	Wealth per capita (U.S.$)
Australia	835,000
Canada	704,000
Luxembourg	658,000
Switzerland	647,000
Japan	565,000
Sweden	496,000
Iceland	486,000
Qatar	473,000
DAE	471,000
Denmark	453,000
Norway	424,000
United States	421,000
France	413,000
Kuwait	405,000
Germany	399,000

Source: The World Bank, 1996

This unique study evaluated 172 countries based on three key "wealth" criteria: natural resources, human resources, and industrial assets. When considering the three factors, Canada's wealth rating was calculated by the World Bank as $488,000 per person in natural resources (69% of the total), $154,000 in human assets (22%), and $60,000 in industrial assets (9%). In contrast, the structure of the American "portfolio of national assets" was significantly different from ours. Natural resources comprised only 25% of their wealth ($105,000 per person), and almost 60% was determined to be in human resources ($252,000). Industrial assets were just over 15% ($63,000).

The second study, the United Nations annual Human Development Report, was released in mid-July, and it ranked Canada as the best place to live - for the third year in a row! Canada was followed by Japan, the United States, Netherlands, and Norway based on wide ranging quality of life, economic growth, and income criteria.

What do these studies tell us? Most obviously, that in the eyes of the rest of the world, we are all very lucky to be Canadians. But, if we follow Bill Gates' advice to "drill down" below obvious conclusions for greater insight, we will find less reason to wallow in complacency.

These studies are, in our opinion, a wake-up call to Canadians. The key to their understanding lies not in what this research says about where Canadians currently rank but rather on how well we are utilizing our ample resources to create wealth for our future.

According to the World Bank, the brightest future belongs to those countries, not necessarily with the greatest wealth, but which make the best use of the wealth they have to create continuing, long-term prosperity. In this regard, human resources (such as creativity, business entrepreneurship, education, health, etc.) and economic productivity, not natural resources, mark the road to the future. In our opinion, this is not necessarily the road Canadians are on because most of our national wealth lies in assets we have, in a sense, "inherited" rather than in assets we have "earned" or created. Is Canada, in the words of one of Canada's most respected novelists, Modecai Richler, "a rich land, populated by lazy people"? I hope not; but it is up to each one of us to help prove otherwise.

Are there any parallels between this situation and lessons we can adapt to the management of our own "portfolio of personal assets?" We think so. We also think that there are special and unique characteristics of this country and its people which individual investors, financial advisors, and product providers must all recognize.

FAILING GRADES

Canadians have always prided themselves in their moderation and community values. In contrast, the United States has always been a country of extremes: in national achievement and failure, in hyperactivity and laziness, in personal conviction and hypocrisy, and in wealth and poverty.

This greater sense of balance and equality among Canadians carries over into our financial life. In

Capitalism Without Capital, Geoffrey Hawthorn points out that in 1960, the richest 1% of American families owned 36% of the pool of private capital in the United States. The next 9% of the population controlled another 36% in private wealth. The remaining 90% of Americans controlled 28% of private capital which means that, at the bottom end, 230 million Americans share roughly $1 trillion in personal assets.

In contrast, in Canada, with its much smaller economy, our population of 30 million people share roughly $1 trillion in personal assets but with a much greater degree of equity than in the United States. Here, the wealthiest 1% of the population control only 10% of Canada's private wealth ($100 billion or so). In fact, there are only about 275,000-300,000 Canadians with annual incomes over $150,000 a year and total assets (including their principal residence) over $1 million.

But even wealthy Canadians have different priorities than wealthy Americans, and in fact, they have been less effective in understanding the need for comprehensive personal financial planning. Almost one-third of Americans with an investment portfolio have a financial plan - in contrast to only 13% of Canadian investors.

Canada's Wealthy vs. U.S. Wealthy

Those who have a...	Canadians	Americans
Will	71%	75%
Estate Plan	41%	44%
Tax Shelter Product	2%	25%
Life Insurance	11%	16%
Independent Advisor	10%	54%

But, let's forget about assets and think instead about our ability to create personal wealth. Is there any evidence that average Canadians are any better off financially than Americans? The evidence is not reassuring. Generally, Canadians and Americans both have a poor knowledge of financial products and the key elements of financial planning. For example:

- a national survey of investor knowledge in the United States concluded that less than 20% of Americans (based on a survey of 1,001 investors by the Investor Protection Trust) have a basic under standing of financial terms and the ways various financial products work;

- two out of three investors, particularly women and seniors, don't have personal financial plans, and 90% of investors had never checked out the credentials and disciplinary history of their broker or advisor;

- when *Money* magazine and Vanguard Funds Group developed a questionnaire of twenty basic questions on mutual funds and investing and surveyed 1,467 people, less than half of the questions, on average, were answered correctly (the average score was 49%; 52% for men and 43% for women).

In Canada, an Angus Reid poll taken earlier this year found that:

- Canadians felt that they need to become better, more knowledgeable investors if they are going to have enough money to retire on. In fact, just over 50% stated that it had to be their highest priority;

- the most common reasons potential investors gave for not seeking professional advice were that they were not sure about their obligations, the cost of services, and the impartiality of the counsel they would be receiving.

What does this tell us? To be blunt, that at best, millions of investors (and especially women and retired seniors) are sadly lacking in the knowledge required to manage their personal finances effectively, and, at worse, they are sitting ducks for investment fraud and abuse.

TAKING CHARGE

So how can you improve your knowledge? Here are some basic guidelines which transcend geographic borders:

1. Learn about different types of investments. Often your motivation will be better if you do it together with a friend or two.

2. Bone up on the basics about how to evaluate investment returns. Don't be afraid of asking your advisor questions, even stupid ones.

3. Familiarize yourself with the various factors that affect financial risk and reward. Brush up on fundamental investing strategies by doing a little bit of reading.

4. Understand that financial planning is not necessarily expensive, time consuming, or only for wealthy people. In fact, it is more important for average Canadians.

5. Be prepared to share personal financial information with your advisor. Once you have selected an advisor, allow them to do their job and don't handcuff them by withholding complete knowledge of your financial situation.

But what about those Canadians who are currently receiving professional advice to help them manage their financial affairs? A recent Canadian study by the Gallop research organization (see below) revealed the ranking of the most common sources of investment advice.

Interestingly, according to this Gallop study, ordinary Canadians very rarely had more than one financial advisor, unlike wealthy Canadians who quite often had several.

These findings were substantiated by our own "What the Rich Do" research which formed the basis of our book of the same title.

Interestingly, men and women have very different approaches to the learning process and identifying sources of information they most rely upon.

Taking Financial Advice

Women, more than men, trust their spouses for investment advice.

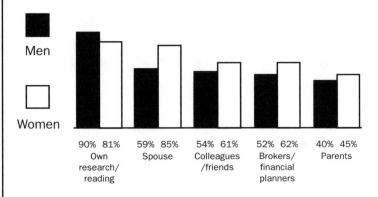

Men

Women

90% 81%	59% 85%	54% 61%	52% 62%	40% 45%
Own research/ reading	Spouse	Colleagues /friends	Brokers/ financial planners	Parents

People who believe these are "very" or "somewhat" important sources of education about investing.

Source: Prudential Securities survey of adults with at least $50,000 household income

Information Source	Average Canadian	Wealthy Canadian
bank, trust company or credit union	34%	10%
financial planners	21%	46%
accountants	20%	22%
insurance agents	15%	0%
lawyers	6%	7%
brokers	4%	47%

FAMILY FINANCE - GET A GRIP!

So, are there any differences in the financial profile of Canadian families compared to American families? You bet. The most obvious difference is that historically Canadians have always been great savers. This is still true, but the recession has been brutal for most Canadians. Between 1992 and 1994, the savings rate for Canadians declined from over 10% of income to less than 6% and even lower (roughly 2.5%) for women (who should be saving 15% of their income prior to age sixty and 20% after). In contrast, the American savings rate has suffered a long-term decline from around 7% in the 1960s to less than 4% today.

In the United States, stocks and bonds together now account for 75% of the total value of a typical family's assets according to a recent study conducted by the Federal Reserve Bank of Kansas City. Equities specifically make up one-third of total household financial assets, and mutual fund holdings are now 12% of all equity holdings (up from 3% in 1980).

In Canada, according to an Ernst & Young study, 30% of Canadian adults hold some of their assets in mutual funds (roughly equivalent to the United States), but when comparing those with funds the average Canadian holding of $49,000 (Canadian) is only half the value of an American's $74,000 (American).

At the bottom end of the scale, poverty rates are significantly lower in Canada than in the United States.

Poverty Rates		
Those living in poverty	Canada	U.S.
Under age 18	9%	21%
18-65	7%	10%
65+	3%	11%

Although debt levels are extraordinarily high in both countries, there are also some important differences. Canadians are typically much more debt averse than Americans, but this is also changing.

In the United States, outstanding credit card debt grew by 40% between 1993 and 1995 to a total of $380 billion while Canadian credit card debt has been increasing in aggregate by 2%-3% per year. By the end of 1995 total U.S. consumer debt (unsecured by real estate) amounted to $1.15 trillion compared to about $450 billion in Canada. To put this into perspective, American consumers on average were paying 11% of gross income servicing their debt.

Bankruptcy rates also are illustrative. Statistics Canada shows that for 1995, consumer bankruptcies climbed 22% to a record high of 65,432 (2.21 for every 1,000 Canadians, which is more than double 1980's level). In addition, business bankruptcies rose 12% to the third highest level ever to 13,258 (1.43 for every 100 businesses).

In contrast, in the United States, Tennessee, Georgia, and Alabama had the highest rate of personal bankruptcies (each at well over 6 per every 1,000), and the U.S. average is 3.29 per 1,000 - 50% higher than Canadian rates.

Again differences are illustrative of the different financial psychology at work. In Canada, the debt burden is a function of a slow, yet consistent, growth of debt based on ill-advised consumer spending. In contrast, research by the American firm SMR Research of Budd Lake, New Jersey, found that in the United States bankruptcy was much more closely related to a major "insolvency event" (for example, an uninsured auto accident, lack of adequate medical insurance, divorce proceedings, or the failure of a self-owned business).

This difference may be explained by a much more pervasive "risk tolerance" by Americans by not preparing themselves financially to face adverse events. Also, Canadians seem to be more comfortable with consumer spending technology than Americans. For example:

- with 26 million debit cards in circulation in Canada, each card was used an average 15.2 times by Canadians in 1995 versus only 3.5 times for Americans;

- in 1994 Canadians used bank ATMs an average of forty-one times versus only thirty-one times for Americans;

- in Canada, the number of debt card transactions jumped from 393 million in 1994 to roughly 700 million in 1995, twice the rate of increase in the United States.

INVESTMENT STRATEGY - PSYCHOLOGICALLY SPEAKING

It is generally acknowledged that Canadian investors have a much more conservative investment strategy than Americans. For example, most Canadian investors structure their portfolios around a much greater proportion of fixed income investments (such as GICs, T-Bills, and Money Market accounts) than Americans. Canadians also are more likely to view their investment portfolio as long-term money. In contrast, Americans are more likely to throw money into the market - only to find they need it later for living expenses, which forces them to sell to raise cash.

Americans also tend to be more aggressive "sector" investors (such as high-technology and biotechnology) - probably looking for the "home run" rather than patient long-term accumulation of capital. It is true that sector investments can make big gains when the market does well, but recent experience has shown these investments also can fall the fastest on the downside.

With the exception of a small group of direct sales, no-load mutual fund companies (such as Altamira, Phillips, Hager & North, and Scudder), most Canadians purchase funds through intermediaries such as bank branches, full-service brokerages, mutual fund dealers, or independent financial planners. In the United States, more often than in Canada, a greater proportion of mutual fund sales are made directly to the public without the involvement of a professional advisor or the benefit of their advice.

In fact, University Avenue Management Limited (the

prime mover behind the No-Load Mutual Fund Alliance in Canada several years ago) announced in September it is largely abandoning its strategy of selling mutual funds directly to the Canadian public. It is only the most recent example of a continuing trend in Canada away from a direct sales approach. New load-charging firms, such as G.T. Global Canada and O'Donnell Fund Management Limited, have been success stories, in comparison to the difficulties experienced by Scudder Canada (a New York based no-load fund which recently launched in Canada) and the stalled growth of Altamira.

With a greater reliance on direct sales, Americans often have a more short-term focus and "trading" philosophy which leads to a quicker decision to "dump" funds during market corrections.

Even though Canadians tend to be slow learners, evidence suggests that once the message sinks in, Canadians are more consistent and committed investors than Americans. This can be seen in the recent example of stock market turmoil in July. While the U.S. based Investment Company Institute reported that the flow of American money into U.S. equity mutual funds dropped by 75% (June and July) when markets were highly volatile, a survey of major Canadian fund companies by the Financial Post reported continued steady inflows into equity funds by Canadians.

Distinct differences exist even within Canada. While the vast majority of Canadians have little or no exposure to global equities, significant investors are more global than Americans. June 30 data from the Investment Funds Institute of Canada showed that

Canadians have roughly $30 billion in global equity funds and only $4.5 billion in U.S. equity funds (a ratio of greater than 6:1). Although comparative data for the U.S. is not available, Americans are much more focussed on NYSE and NASDAQ stocks than international stocks or exchanges. The overall ratio of international versus domestic equity investments for Americans is much closer to 1:1. However, there are signs this may be changing; $20 billion was invested globally in the first half of 1996 by Americans - triple the amount for all of 1995.

Mutual Funds by Generation

The new report on mutual fund ownership shows slight differences in how generations invest.

Generation (age)	Stock funds	Bond and income funds	Money market funds	Not specified
Generation X (19-31)	37%	29%	31%	3%
Baby Boom (32-50)	49%	20%	26%	4%
Silent Generation (51-71)	59%	23%	13%	5%
GI Generation (72-92)	45%	32%	23%	0%

Source: *Investment Company Institute*

THE BABY BOOM BUST - WHAT HAPPENED?

Much has been written about the prosperity and financial well-being of the Baby Boom generation. Unfortunately, we now see quite a different picture - The Baby Boom Bust.

The purpose of presenting our research on The Baby Boom Bust is not to cast a negative pallor over the country but to present a factual state of where Canadians are financially, and what the prudent consumer/investor can and should do about it.

Nineteen ninety-seven is year three of a ten-year consumer recession. This is not an overall economic recession of quarter after quarter negative Gross Domestic Product numbers. In fact, a low dollar will continue to stimulate strong export sales which constitute 38% of the economy. However, consumer expenditures are 60% of economic activity and they will show little, if any, growth for the next decade.

The reality is that many of the best investment opportunities often can be found during difficult economic times. It is our view that there will be just as much financial and investment opportunity over the next nine-year period as ever before. Perhaps even more. Financial and mutual fund stocks will do exceedingly well, as will oil & gas shares, new technology, software, and Internet companies. On the other hand, consumer stocks will lag as will manufacturers of durables, cars, and homes. Retail malls, office towers, and big city markets will suffer, as well as "fixed income only" investors facing low returns. Owners of GICs will suffer a major loss of purchasing power and capital.

Here are the ten factors that we discovered and led us to believe that this is year three of a ten-year consumer recession. Govern yourself accordingly.

1. *Earned Income:*

Average family income declined by 3.4% last year to levels in line with 1984. Taxes continue to rise as a percentage of income because there is no indexing of income tax credits and deductions as inflation remains less than 3%.

2. *Taxes:*

Average family taxes from federal, provincial, and municipal sources is now 46.5% of total income.

3. *Savings:*

Personal savings in 1997 will decline to 5.8% of disposable income from 10.5% in 1990. Consumers have no money to spend.

4. *Debt:*

Personal indebtedness has increased from 62% of assets in 1992 to 93% in 1996. Consumers are buried in debt.

5. *Salary:*

Salary increases are largely nonexistent and many companies are trying to hold costs down. They are cutting benefits and pensions, especially government.

6. *Unearned Income:*

Income from savings and investments are down 20% from 1993 levels because of the reliance on fixed income products.

7. Jobs:

Job loss continues in both the private and public sectors at unprecedented levels. People afraid of job security do not buy. The only growth in employment is in self-employment, home business, and part-time service jobs. Most of those losing jobs are in their peak earning years.

8. Government:

Federal and provincial cost cutting passes costs and tax liabilities to municipalities, causing a property tax increase which adds further pressure to the downward spiral of real estate prices, the principal portfolio asset of most Canadians.

9. Demographics:

Canada's aging population needs less and buys less clothing, food, housing, cars, and entertainment. They are now confronted with the double challenge of supporting aging parents living on government assistance and children aged sixteen to twenty-nine with limited job prospects and earnings potential.

10. Inheritance:

As the Boomers confront these challenges, those over sixty with 65% of the disposable income and savings are living longer and are relying even more on their personal investments for income. Three-quarters of all Baby Boomers will inherit only debts from their parents, not the $1 trillion expected over the next ten years. It is concentrated in the hands of only one-third of the elderly and has declined to $600 billion because of the declining value of fixed income securities and real estate values.

THE BABY BOOM BUST -
WHERE DO WE GO FROM HERE?

Our national study on those Canadians born in the period from 1946 to 1960 has shown us some interesting characteristics.

Baby Boomer Characteristics

78% own their own home
56% have a family income of $40,000 or greater
45% are satisfied with their financial situation
47% claim to be in good personal shape
53% have a high school education or less
93% have been or are married
73% are now married
69% have two or more children
69% have two or more wage earners in the house
30% have less than $2,000 in savings & investments
29% $10,000 to $149,000 in savings
13% have $150,000 to $500,000
1% have over a million dollars
18% of men in this group and 33% of women will live to 90

Here are the ten factors that Baby Boomers must deal with as they age.

1. Work:
Assume that your formal working life may last only

to age fifty-eight, not sixty-five. You do not have fifteen more years of earnings for retirement. Corporate cost cutting and downsizing may reduce compulsory retirement to age sixty and early retirement is now age fifty-five. The problem is that you will live an average of ten to fifteen years longer than your parents did.

2. *The Social Safety Net:*

Do not count on it for much. Only the most destitute will receive it. Today, 82% of all women over sixty-five rely totally on government assistance for their income. This is a luxury of the past. CPP is insolvent. Premiums will rise to one-tenth of total salary. OAS is now subject to withholding taxes. Universality is dead and personal responsibility is in.

3. *Retirement and Company Pensions:*

In 1997, you need 75% of the average of your best five years of salary to maintain your lifestyle. In 2005, you will need 100% of your best five years. Company pensions are set at 60%. Most are fixed to real estate and mortgage portfolios that experienced a sharp decline in value. Many companies are cutting retirement and pension benefits. You will need to save 15% of gross earnings if you are male and 20% if your are female to have a secure retirement. This is three times the current rate of saving.

4. Inheritance:

Do not count on it. Two-thirds of parents will die

leaving only debts. The $1 trillion expected to be inherited in the next ten years in the hands of the "Lucky Sperm Club" has declined in value to $600 billion because of poor investments and declining real estate values.

5. *Estate Planning:*

Everyone sixty years of age or older needs a will, a power of attorney, and a personal care proxy.

6. *Responsibilities:*

The Boomers need not only worry about themselves but also about their parents and their children. The Boomers are the sandwich generation. Their parents are outliving their investment income, and the Generation X kids refuse to leave home. Some even have to care for grandparents and their own grandchildren.

7. *Insurance:*

While Boomers with grown children will need little life insurance to protect income, they will need it for the second family if they are remarried, as well as for estate planning. Premiums will continue to rise because of diseases like AIDS.

8. *Relationships:*

Breaking up will be harder to do than ever and certainly more expensive. CPP, RRSPs, pensions, and savings must be split up between spouses. Both partners lose income and assets and will end up poorer. If at all possible, stay together or face poverty.

9. *Stress:*

Boomers are already overwhelmed with it. Many chose self-fulfillment, leisure, and the self-expression approach to cope with it but are now having to deal with career, aging, family, and lifestyle stress along with financial pressures. Defeatism and pessimism now dominates Boomer thinking.

10. *Spending and Personal Goals:*

Credit cards and cash machines have destroyed the Boomers' savings. It is not too late to change your life and your goals. Use financial planning software to track your money and reconsider your priorities. Being fifty is a lot younger than it used to be.

Financial Planning

"Knowledge is the greatest competitive advantage of the 1990s; knowledge without action is nothing."

WHAT IS FINANCIAL PLANNING?

Proper financial planning is a comprehensive, logical, and ongoing system for managing your finances to achieve personal objectives based on the *"Group of Seven."* A complete personal financial plan incorporates seven key elements:

1. Effectively managing daily family expenses

2. Building a portfolio of investments

3. Minimizing personal income taxes

4. Securing your retirement by protecting your income and assets from unforeseen and unfavourable circumstances

5. Preparing an estate plan

6. Regularly updating your powers of attorney

7. Regularly updating your personal will

WHAT DO THE RICH DO?

Why is it that wealthy Canadians are wealthy? Usually, it is for one of two reasons: They were lucky or they have worked very, very hard. If they are lucky, they may have been born into a wealthy family or they may have won a lottery. However, people who fall into the "lucky" category represent less than 5% of all those people which are research identified as "rich." The other 95% — they worked for their success. So what can we learn from wealthy Canadians? Our research shows that they do three things better than most people.

1. They have a well thought out and consistent strategy for managing their money.

87% have a retirement plan
70% have an estate plan
94% have a will

2. They accept that they need the assistance of at least one (and often several) professional advisors.

35% consult at least one professional advisor regularly
70% seek other sources of independent financial information
59% subscribe to financial magazines and newsletters

3. They have discipline.

*55% update their financial plan more than
once a year
87% contribute to an RRSP every year*

However, each of these three characteristics can be learned by anyone if you are prepared to make the effort. In the long run, you will find it pays off handsomely.

WHY IS FINANCIAL PLANNING IMPORTANT?

In Canada in the 1990s, you are increasingly responsible for your own financial well-being. No one else is going to look after you. Financial planning is important because it is the only way you have of protecting yourself and your family from the growing economic threats to your wealth we are seeing in Canada. Prudent financial planning is the only way of significantly improving your financial security and lifestyle. The world of money is increasingly complex, and you need greater knowledge in order to more effectively manage your money. Financial planning will force you to think about your future and to take charge. The secret to financial success is being proactive, not reactive.

The *first step* is to think about, and clearly define, your financial goals and objectives in life. Without knowing your ultimate destination, it is difficult to know what road to take. Therefore, you must decide how important such things as lifestyle, housing, education, income, leisure activities, employment satisfaction, and financial security for your family are to you and what commitments you must make to reach these goals.

Once you understand what your goals and objectives are, the **second step** is to spend some time documenting and understanding what we call your financial inventory. This time is well spent to help you identify your current financial situation. It tells you what you've got to work with. This process includes valuing your assets, identifying your debts, describing your income (and where it comes from), and classifying your expenses.

The **third step** in creating a personal financial plan is to seek the assistance of a professional financial advisor to help you. It takes a very special and talented person with lots of time on their hands to be able to manage their finances properly and effectively — completely on their own. A professional advisor will explain the financial planning process, help you find the time to do it, identify products and strategies appropriate for your situation, assist you to make complicated financial decisions, and monitor and update your plan on a regular basis.

Once you have done these three things, you are well on your way to taking control of your money!

HOW TO SELECT A FINANCIAL ADVISOR

"Eighty-one percent of Canadians want knowledge and education from their advisors."

The most frequently asked question I get at seminars and through the mail is how do you tell a good financial advisor from a poor one.

The first issue is to determine what type of advisor you need, if any. Are you a sophisticated and experienced investor who knows exactly what you want and why? Do you have substantial experience in investing and a track record of success? If the answer to these questions is yes, then you probably are similar to about 5% of Canadians who use a discount broker or buy your mutual funds direct. The big issue for this group is getting the lowest cost of acquisition, as they need little advice or planning.

Another 10-30% are knowledgeable investors who need the services of a broker. You are getting a degree of financial advice and information, but your threshold of decision making is higher and you need a sophisticated advisor. You should look for one who has good references, has years of experience, and can provide a broad array of products from bonds to equities to mutual funds and will provide regular economic and financial reports and briefings.

Our research shows that over the past thirty-six months, those who had the benefits of a independent financial advisor had returns 34% higher than those who tried to do it all themselves. More than 50% of the population is best served by a fully qualified experienced independent financial planner.

You should look for one who has professional distinctions such as being a certified or chartered financial planner. References are also important as well as proven financial performance. Personal compatibility is important as well as a clear understanding of your goals and objectives. The intent is to find someone who you can trust and work with long term, a true financial confidant.

A good financial planner will prepare a comprehensive financial plan which will include an investment plan, tax plan, retirement plan, and estate plan as needed. They will not just sell you mutual funds in the first meeting.

Make sure your advisor is truly independent and can gain access to any of the over 1,400 mutual funds and 60 fixed income products available in the market today. Many claim to be independent and only offer 5 or 6 options.

Find out right from the beginning what the advisor will charge and how they are compensated. It's your choice today, not the advisors. You can pay on a deferred basis if you hold the funds for at least six years and end up paying nothing for the advice.

What is important is that you decide what category you are in and get the right advisor as soon as possible. Remember, the right advisor does make the difference.

The decision on who should advise you is extremely important, affecting your risk, rates of return, access to investment products, information flow, and long-term security. It is very much a shopping experience; and it pays to interview several potential candidates. Here are the criteria that I feel are the most critical:

1. **Qualifications:**
   Licenses by a securities commission, or carrying one of several professional designations such as certified or chartered financial planner, financial analyst, or chartered life underwriter, are obviously an advantage.

2. **Experience:**

How long have they worked in the industry and how well do they understand how it works and what is needed to make you more financially secure?

3. References:
Will they provide names of current clients who endorse the performance and service level the advisor provides?

4. Service Level:
Do they offer the types of services, reporting, seminars, education, etc. that you feel are necessary to keep yourself in control of your finances?

5. Availability:
How accessible is the advisor for regular financial reviews?

6. Independence:
Can they access a broad market range of products that will reduce risk, preserve capital, and enhance long-term returns?

7. Knowledge:
Is the advisor familiar with and understanding of people like yourself, your needs, and your lifestyle?

8. Compatibility:
Do you like them and are you comfortable discussing your financial affairs with them openly and honestly?

Here, then, are the basic questions to start your search:

1. What credentials do you have to practice financial planning? What is your education and experience?

2. Are you licensed with a securities commission and what type of licenses do you have?

3. What kind of service will you provide? Will you prepare a complete financial plan and manage my investments for me?

4. How often will you update my plan or give me reports on my investments?

5. How will you get paid? Do you charge a flat fee or a percentage of the portfolio value? Do you accept commissions from companies for selling their products? Do I have a choice in the ways I purchase?

6. What kind of clients do you have? Will you give me references?

While selecting a financial advisor is not an exact science, there are proven ways to ensure greater satisfaction. Use the above method, criteria, and questions.

BAILING OUT OF DEBT

Canadians are carrying more than $468 billion of debt and are borrowing at credit card rates of 16.95% to

28%. This has led many on the path to financial ruin. How do you bail yourself out of debt when you feel swamped? Remember, we have ninety-three cents of debt for every dollar of assets.

Here are some basic points that may work for you or a friend in trouble:

1. If your total monthly payments on personal, short-term debts, including car loans, bank and department store credit cards but excluding your mortgage, is over 20% of your total payments, you may be in over your head. It should not be more than 6-7%.

2. Resolve to pay until it hurts. Add up your total debts and payments and budgets and determine the maximum that you can afford to spend on debt payments. A goal should be to commit up to 25% of net cash flow to pay off your debts. Then resolve to change your spending habits. This means a discipline that will last for several years if any debt reduction will take place.

3. Establish priorities. If you have substantial department store debt at 28%, it will take ten to twenty years to pay it off if you pay only the mini mum balance each month. As this is the most expensive debt, it should be paid down first and the savings on the interest will be greater.

4. Get in touch with creditors. If you can't meet

minimum payment requirements, get in touch with creditors and let them know what you can do. They will not forgive loans, but they may waive later penalties and allow you to stretch the payments out if you stay regular.

5. Refinance the total package. Consolidating all of your debt into one package at a lower rate may be a better option. A second mortgage at 9% is cheaper than a credit card at 17%. Don't borrow from your RRSP, but restructure your total cash flow so you have only one payment each month. Then hide or destroy your cards to avoid a further run up. This is a good strategy if you change your habits.

6. Get good help. There are many credit counselling agencies available in your community. Some are social service agencies or community groups that provide the service at a low charge. They will contact credit grantors and arrange for a personal budget. The counselling is a valuable service. Many firms operate loan counselling services, then charge you $500 for the service, leaving you even poorer. This is not a good idea.

The best way to avoid bad debt and a cash flow crunch is not to build bad habits or live on plastic. Too many people borrow on one card to pay off another. This is no way to live.

If you are in financial trouble, face it head on and fol-

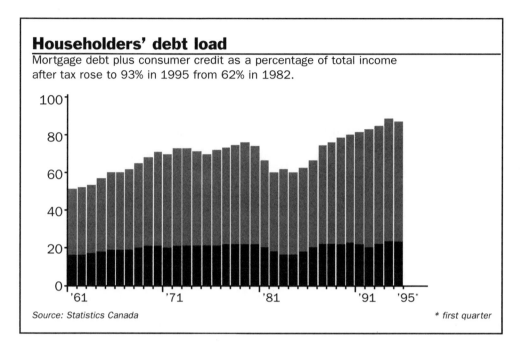

Householders' debt load

Mortgage debt plus consumer credit as a percentage of total income after tax rose to 93% in 1995 from 62% in 1982.

Source: Statistics Canada   * first quarter

low the six-point plan. It can help you and offer a light at the end of the debt tunnel.

WHY OWNING MAY STILL BE BETTER THAN RENTING

Perhaps you are concerned that home values in your area have declined in recent years. Unless you bought at the market peak in 1988-89, you can still come out on top. Because of leverage, borrowing via a mortgage to finance your home may still be a viable investment. If you paid $300,000 for your home and put 30% down and prices rise 2%, the return is $6,000 tax free on $90,000 — a 6.7% return.

In fact, over the past decade, the average annual

return on real estate has been 7.1% versus 4.1% after-tax yield on fixed income securities.

Every situation and community is different. For a more complete comparison, suppose that instead of buying a house, you rent and invest the down payment. Then every year you invest the amount by which ownership costs such as mortgage payments, property taxes, and maintenance would exceed your rental outlay.

If over time by following this strategy, you could accumulate wealth more quickly by renting your home than you would by owning, then you made the right choice by renting. Our comparison assumes the homeowner has an average 30% tax rate and the renter can earn an average and conservative 7% on his money after tax. The renter, we'll assume, pays annual rent at a realistic 8% of the home's value while our homeowner has property maintenance, and tax costs of 2.3%.

Over a ten-year period, the benefit of owning a home exceeds the benefit of renting if home values rise at least 2% annually. If the renter's return on investment is higher, say 10% after tax, the owner still wins at 3% appreciation. The owner's part of the gain is completely tax free. He can deduct many household expenses such as insurance, tax, and heat from home business income and can use the house as an asset to leverage against for investment purposes.

When the mortgage is paid off, the owner's costs drop sharply while the renter's costs keep going up.

Of course, this model is general. Rents in your area may be lower or you may have purchased at the peak of the market or when interest rates were higher. With no price appreciation, the situation does change.

If there is a message here, it is that in most markets with modest price appreciation, it is better to buy. However, don't buy the most expensive house you can afford using all of your capital. Buy a good house, but set money aside for investments in stocks, mutual funds, and good quality bonds. Roll as much as possible into your RRSP each year for you and your spouse, and use the tax refunds to pay down the mortgage.

WHY IS NO ONE SAVING ANYMORE?

In these remarkable times of government cutbacks, clawbacks, and tax increases, why are Canadians reducing their level of personal savings? This is a time for maximum thrift and careful conservation of cash to ensure a reasonable chance at a safe retirement. In the last twelve months, personal savings rates have dropped from 10.5% of disposable income to 8.5%, and these rates are even lower for women. Women under fifty average savings rates as low as 2.5% at a time that they should be saving 15%, which in turn should rise to 20% of income by the age of sixty.

The average Canadian retiree lives on five sources of income: 46% rely nearly entirely on government assistance programs such as OAS or the Guaranteed Income Supplement; 37% receive some form of corporate pension; about 18% still must work after age sixty-five full- or part-time; and only about 30% report relying substantially on personal savings and investments.

Married Couples	Target saving rate for ages			
	25-35	35-44	45-54	55-64
Earnings=$30,000				
with pension	0.3%	4.6%	12.0%	11.5%
without pension	2.3	11.4	18.2	17.7
Earnings=$50,000				
with pension	0.7	6.3	16.6	15.9
without pension	3.0	11.8	21.5	20.8
Earnings=$75,000				
with pension	1.2	8.3	20.1	19.1
without pension	4.0	14.1	25.1	24.2
Earnings=$100,000				
with pension	3.9	8.8	17.6	24.7
without pension	7.8	15.4	23.5	30.1
Earnings=$150,000				
with pension	5.6	11.8	20.6	28.9
without pension	10.2	19.4	27.4	34.9

Single Men	Target saving rate for ages			
	25-35	35-44	45-54	55-64
Earnings=$30,000				
with pension	1.0%	8.3%	13.5%	12.3%
without pension	4.2	16.4	21.0	19.7
Earnings=$50,000				
with pension	0.5	7.9	19.2	16.1
without pension	4.0	16.9	27.1	24.1
Earnings=$75,000				
with pension	2.4	9.8	17.5	23.7
without pension	7.9	20.2	26.9	32.3
Earnings=$100,000				
with pension	3.5	12.2	20.1	26.9
without pension	9.6	23.2	30.0	35.9
Earnings=$150,000				
with pension	5.7	16.6	21.7	38.3
without pension	11.8	28.4	32.8	38.3

	Target saving rate for ages			
Single Women	**25-35**	**35-44**	**45-54**	**55-64**
Earnings=$30,000				
with pension	8.2%	10.0%	11.4%	12.2%
without pension	12.7	17.2	18.5	19.0
Earnings=$50,000				
with pension	10.0	9.6	12.4	17.2
without pension	15.9	18.2	20.7	24.9
Earnings=$75,000				
with pension	11.9	13.2	16.9	22.1
without pension	18.5	22.2	25.5	30.0
Earnings=$100,000				
with pension	13.7	15.9	19.8	25.2
without pension	20.6	25.1	28.5	33.2
Earnings=$150,000				
with pension	16.5	20.0	22.0	28.4
without pension	23.3	30.4	32.1	37.6

Old Age Security was available only at age seventy in 1965 and then was reduced to age sixty-five and soon will likely follow the U.S. model rising back up to age sixty-nine by 1999.

Higher taxes and lower wage increases make saving more difficult, so we are now in a period of substantial "dissaving," using credit cards with massive frequency and increasing personal debt to unheard of levels.

Most women under forty report great difficulty having an adequate aftertax cash flow to be able to save. For a single parent head of household this is nearly impossible.

This process of economic transformation makes it certain that we will have to work longer, live on less, and spend less at a time when most traditional sources of retirement income will be heading downward.

Saving for the future

Financial assets of women aged forty-five to fifty-four by personal income, 1991

	Number of workers* ('000)	Proportion of workers with		
		Employer-sponsored pension plans	RRSPs	Other Investments**
All women aged 45-54	654	52	67	40
Less than $20,000	290	28	52	31
$20,000-$39,000	277	68	79	42
$40,000-$59,999	64	89	90	60
$60,000 and over	23	57	60	79

* Excludes respondents who did not disclose personal income information

** Includes property bought for investment purposes and financial instruments such as stocks and bonds.

Source: Statistics Canada

Are there any serious options to consider?

1. Establish a daily cash summary of all expenditures down to $1.00 to determine your spending pattern over ninety days.

2. Identify and eliminate impulse buying and focus on cash conservation at all costs.

3. Use your cash savings to profit maximize. Consider Treasury Bills once you have $1,000 or more in the bank and avoid daily interest accounts or chequing accounts with low or no returns.

4. Consider money market mutual funds for shorter term cash.

5. Invest to maximize capital growth while you are under sixty and only moderately reduce this pattern as you get older.

6. Pay credit card balances on time and consider the new debit cards to spend only what you have.

7. Hold cars longer and plan all capital outlays for appliances and furniture well in advance. Price is the thing in the 1990s.

8. Alter the amortization of your mortgage downward to reduce nondeductible interest expense and ensure a faster payoff.

9. Renew mortgages and refinance on interest rate downturns or preferably stay variable to maximize the short-term rate advantage.

10. Focus on clear retirement income objectives totalling all your sources and what standard you wish to maintain. Maximize all retirement income contributions and ensure each spouse has a separate plan.

Saving in the 1990s is not impossible, it just requires a lot more effort and strategy, and regardless of how difficult it is you have no choice.

We now have twenty-two cents in debt for every dollar of disposable income. Americans have eighteen cents per dollar. We just can't afford to go any higher.

YOUR FINANCIAL IQ:
How Much Do You Know?

What do you know about the fundamentals of personal finance? Most people know less than they think. The lack of knowledge is a major factor in the failure to achieve financial success. Give yourself ten points for each correct answer. The total is 120.

1. Over the past seventy years which of the following investments overwhelmingly earned more than the other two?
   a. five-year GICs
   b. real estate
   c. stocks

2. Over the past twenty-five years which of the following investment strategies was the least likely to experience swings in value called volatility?
   a. 100% Government of Canada bonds (long term ten years)
   b. 70% large company Canadian stocks and 30% mid term (five-year/Government of Canada bonds)
   c. 30% small company Canadian stocks and 70% large company Canadian stocks

3. When interest rates rise, bond prices
   a. rise
   b. fall
   c. neither, interest rate moves do not directly affect bond prices

4. You invest $1,000 in a stock. After one year the stock price falls 20%. The next year the price jumps 20%. After two years you have
    a. broken even
    b. made money
    c. lost money

5. When selecting a mutual fund, it is important that you
    a. evaluate the funds five-year past performance record
    b. pick a fund that meets your investment goals
    c. pick a fund run by a well-respected manager
    d. pick a fund with low fees

6. It is safer to buy a mutual fund from a bank than from a brokerage firm. True or false?

7. You cannot lose money you invest in a money market mutual fund. True or false?

8. Any wage earner can contribute some money to an RRSP. True or false?

9. Interest paid on a home equity line of credit is tax deductible.
    a. always
    b. sometimes
    c. never

10. If you give $10,000 or more in cash to a relative or child, it is subject to a gift tax. True or false?

11. Assuming the average Canadian consumer owes $3,500 in credit card debt, at an average rate of interest of 18%, how long will it take to pay off the debt if the minimum monthly payment is made?

    a. seven years
    b. four years
    c. twelve years
    d. fifteen years

12. Which of the following life insurance products is best if you want the largest immediate tax-free death benefit for the lowest possible cost?

    a. universal life
    b.   term life
    c. whole life

ANSWERS

1. (c) Stocks have returned the highest.

2. (b) The portfolio of five-year bonds and large company stocks is roughly one-third as volatile as long-term bonds and half as volatile as a large company, small company plan. This is called asset allocation.

3. (b) Producing a capital loss.

4. (c) You lost money. You need a 25% gain to break even.

5. (b)

6. False. Unlike deposits and GICs, the $60,000 guarantee does not apply.

7. False. They are not guaranteed but rarely is any money ever lost in them.

8. False. This can happen if your private pension plan

contribution leaves no additional room to top up with your RRSP as reflected on your Pension Adjustment Statement.

9. (b) Sometimes, as when it is borrowed for investment purposes, the interest expense is deductible.

10. False. There is no gift tax in Canada.

11. (d) But increase the monthly payment by $10 and it drops to four years.

12. (b) Term policies pay only a basic death benefit. Whole and universal life build cash value in addition to the death benefit.

SCORE

90-120: You are financially intelligent and on top of what's happening.

60-80: You are financially average and need to educate yourself more.

Less than 60: Boy, are you in need of a lot of help.

Where Canadian's Have Their Money

Source: Bank of Canada Statistical Review, December 1995

		Pre-tax 1997 Average return
Money market funds	$19 billion	2.0%
Canada savings bonds	$31.5 billion	5.5%
Chequing accounts	$80.7 billion	0.0%
Savings accounts	$64.2 billion	0.5%
Term deposits & GICs		
1 year or less	$62.6 billion	2.5%
over 1 year	$250 billion	5.0%

$199 billion of GICs in RRSPs
Canadians now have $210 billion in mutual funds

Real Returns on GICs	
Average return on GICs - 1970s	+ 9.10%
net return after tax and inflation	- 3.12%
Average return on GICs - 1980s	+ 11.40%
net return after tax and inflation	- 0.89%
Average return on GICs - 1996	+ 4.50%
net return after tax and inflation	+ 0.78%

Source: Royal Bank of Canada - December 1996

DOUBLING YOUR NET WORTH

Is it possible to double your net worth every five years? Is this an important objective for you? The rich follow this as a target.

With increasing life expectancy, government cutbacks in social programs, a proposed new senior's benefit program (the substance of which remains mostly unknown), and growing awareness of the poor returns associated with traditional fixed income products such as GICs and Canada Savings Bonds, Canadians have reason for concern. The inescapable reality is that we will all need dynamic income growth for many more years than we have anticipated. Equities will be necessary in every portfolio until at least age seventy-five (although in declining proportion with increasing age). Consider this:

- On average, we have a greater likelihood of living longer than our parents.

- Family disposable income has declined by 5.2% since 1993.

- The Canada Pension Plan is a financial mess.

- We can expect to pay $750 million more in taxes in 1996 than in 1995.

- The 1996 Federal Budget reduced RRSP contribution room by $31,000 in total.
- The new senior's benefit will reduce income for a couple over age sixty-five (with combined income of $68,000) by $3,200 in 2001 or increase taxes by $2,100.

What every Canadian now needs is aggressive income growth. So what is a reasonable expectation? Doubling your net worth every five years is not only possible, but readily attainable for most investors without incurring excessive risk to the capital. Here's why.

Proposition #1: The Bull Market Will Continue

Equity markets will continue to rise over the next ten years and will consistently outperform the returns from both bonds and fixed income securities. Money is driving the market forward.

- Low inflation has made returns on financial assets more attractive than most tangible (hard) assets. For example, the shift in asset allocation by individuals from real estate to stocks will continue.

- Economic growth in most industrialized countries has been weak. The U.S. Federal Reserve continues to lower interest rates, making more money available for financial investments.

- Aging "Baby Boomers" are shifting financial priorities from consumption (houses, cars, raising families, etc.) to a fanatical effort to save and invest for the future.

- As a result of technological innovation, corporate "downsizing," and increased productivity, many companies have been able to generate enormous earnings. Strong businesses don't need money and are not inclined to sell equities. In fact, the trend is to buy back their own outstanding shares.

- The strengthening American and Canadian dollars are attracting more foreign capital into the North American equity markets.

- Mutual fund management firms have large uninvested cash balances from strong sales in 1995-96 which need to be "put to work."

Low interest rates in the G-7 economies are driving

the new flow of funds into the "emerging" markets of Asia and Latin America.

Proposition #2: Asset Allocation Is Key

Remember, your choice of asset allocation within your portfolio is more important than the individual investments that you buy. Don't let strategy buzzwords like "market timing," "sector rotation," or "stock picking" cloud your common sense and good judgment. Trying to "time" the market is a fool's game. If market timers are so correct, why aren't more of them rich?

Asset allocation on the other hand, has clear validity. Here are the important principles:

- Your portfolio should be divided into two parts: 80% should be in "soft assets" (financial products like equities, bonds, fixed income products, and cash or its equivalent), and 20% should be in "hard assets" (oil, natural gas, real estate, etc.).

- Asset allocation in soft assets determines between 85% and 91% of the overall performance of your portfolio. You will need equities to continuously outperform inflation and produce lower taxed capital gains and dividends. You will need bonds for capital gains and the lower level of volatility they offer relative to equities. Finally, you will need some cash for short-term needs and the flexibility to grab attractive investment opportunities as they come along. Hard assets, such as oil and gas, generally run counter to the general cycle of the economy. For example, when equity markets suffer declines, hard assets tend to rise in value as investors seek alternatives. Interestingly, there are ways to utilize hard assets to produce a largely tax-free income stream.

Next, we'll look at the elements of a successful investment strategy capable of producing returns which will double your net worth every five years and also significantly reduce both taxes and financial risk.

WEALTH ODYSSEY - DEVELOPING A STRATEGY

We now know that a number of important factors seem to indicate that equity markets will continue to rise in the long term and that asset allocation decisions affect financial returns more than the individual investments you buy. But how can we achieve double digit returns at a lower tax rate?

Proposition #3: The Value of Value Investing

Value investing, combined with some knowledge of market "momentum," will outperform all other strategies over time. Successful investing requires a clear strategy; it is not a random selection of choices. The investment strategy you adopt will affect your cash flow, taxes, retirement income, and estate plan.

"Great business" companies consistently produce higher shareholder value, capital gains, and dividends than cyclical or "hot sector" stocks. Names such as Coca-Cola, Gillette, and Xerox are global firms generating superior growth.

Patience, in addition to being a virtue, is profitable. If you ignore that psychology of the markets and "stay the course" with investments in great businesses with strong brand names, so to will your returns be consistently superior to other strategies. The only error is to not be invested in the market all the time. If we evaluate the great value investors from 1920 to date, they consistently double their asset values every five years or less as the chart below indicates.

Proposition #4: What About Market Momentum?

Research indicates that there is volatility inherent in following a pure momentum strategy. It is true that momentum investors can produce superior returns of 20%-30% per annum over a relatively short period of four to five years. This can be done by investing strictly in front-running companies while they are going through the growth stage of their corporate life cycle. However, it is hard to find any evidence of long-term momentum investing success.

While 20/20 Aggressive Growth and Marathon follow this approach, more consistent results can be achieved by combining the growth orientation of a momentum strategy with a concern for value as well. Wayne Deans of O'Donnell Investment Management and Veronica Hirsch of AGF fall into this category and have established ten-year track records of superior performance to show for it.

Proposition #5: Your Portfolio Will Evolve Over Time

About 70% of your portfolio should remain constant for up to five years to let the managers you have chosen do their work. However, about 30% of a typical value portfolio may be directly affected by short-term changes in interest rates, the Canadian dollar, and tax legislation. For example, if the Canadian dollar weakens and/or taxes rise, you should invest more money in good businesses earning the bulk of their income outside of Canada.

This does not mean you should try to "time the market." Rather, you must learn to anticipate and respond to changes in not only the Canadian but the world economy. Remember, Canada accounts for only 3% of world stock market capitalization. Understand economic factors influencing the performance of your portfolio. You must constantly monitor your portfolio and act when changes may be required.

Fund Manager	Flagship Fund	Annual Growth[1]
John Maynard Keynes	U.K. Building Societies	19% (1920)
Philip Carret	Pioneer Funds	22% (1930)
John Templeton	Templeton Funds	15% (1954)
Warren Buffet	Berkshire Hathaway	23% (1964)
Peter Lynch	Fidelity Magellan	22% (1972)
Charles Brandeis	20/20 World	22% (1974)
Bob Kremball	Trimark	20% (1982)
Jonathan Wellam	AIC	25% (1989)
Bill Kanko - Dina de Geer	Mackenzie Universal	20% (1989)

More fund managers are adopting the value approach. Mackenzie's Ivy Funds and Mario Gabelli of the O'Donnell Investment Management are other examples of a consistent value orientation with a 20 year track record of 20%+ per year returns.

[1] The year in parentheses indicates the year in which each of these great investors established their reputations and launched their run of superior returns.

Proposition #6: How Much in Foreign Assets?

The optimal threshold for doubling your net worth, regardless of your age, is 60% of your portfolio in Canadian assets and 40% of your portfolio in international assets (especially American and Western European).

However, 91% of Canadian investors have no foreign investments, and those that do are grossly under-weighted in U.S. assets (which currently represent roughly 40% of the world stock market capitalization). Emerging markets should be roughly 10% of your portfolio and offer high returns only when the U.S. prime rate is between 6% and 8%. With higher rates, your exposure should be 5% at maximum. If the U.S. prime is under 6%, emerging market assets could be up to 15% of your portfolio.

WEALTH ODYSSEY - LEVERAGING GROWTH

Now, we will look at how to understand risk and the process of accelerating the growth of your portfolio through reasonable and intelligent use of leverage. We will focus on how to borrow to invest and the role of hard assets such as real estate and resource commodities (like oil and gas) within your portfolio.

Proposition #7: Is Leverage Good or Bad?

In determining whether or not you should borrow to invest, you must consider three key factors: the prevailing level of interest rates (as well as the direction), the tax deductibility of interest costs on the loan, and the degree of leverage. As a rule, it makes sense to borrow to invest during periods when interest rates are low, when leverage is manageable, and when interest costs are tax deductible.

If interest rates and tax issues are appropriate and strong investment opportunities exist in conservative "blue chip" equities and mutual funds, it is logical to leverage up to 20% of the value of your net worth based on a 7% prime rate. Most lenders will even accept these as collateral on their loans.

If interest rates drop to, say, a 6% prime rate, you may feel comfortable leveraging up to 30% of your personal net worth. Conversely, if interest rates rise to, say, an 8% prime, then you should reduce your leverage to 15% or less.

With regard to interest cost, if the aftertax cost of money is 6% or greater, start thinking about paying off the loan. At a 6.75% prime in Canada (at the time of writing), the aftertax cost of tax deductible money is only 3.5% or 4.0%, depending on your tax bracket, so borrowing still makes sense.

Proposition #8: Residential Real Estate Will Continue to Underperform

There will not be a major rebound in the residential real estate market in Canada for at least a decade. However, this does not mean that you should sell your home at a loss. It can be used as a hedge by leveraging against the value it does have to produce better returns on other financial assets in your portfolio. This approach will work to offset any decline in the value of your real estate holdings. This is especially important because your home can also be used as a tax shelter because of the deductibility of expenses from income related to a home business.

Remember, however, that good real estate opportunities do exist right now - most notably, offshore real estate held in good quality Real Estate Investment Trusts (REITs) and Real Estate Investment Funds (REIFs) in high growth U.S. markets. These investments can offer capital gain potential, reasonable and consistent income, tax advantages, and the possibility of currency protection.

Proposition #9: Oil & Gas Looks Good

At present, oil & gas is the best performing hard asset - if you avoid junior issues and high risk penny stocks. Instead, focus on either low risk oil & gas developmental partnerships or Royalty Trust units listed on major stock exchanges like the TSE.

1. Developmental partnerships can produce 100% tax write-offs, capital gains potential, and tax-free income for four years (payable quarterly).

2. Royalty Trusts are liquid, are traded on major stock exchanges, qualify for RRSPs, provide

currency protection (they are denominated in U.S. dollars), and provide tax-free income up to five years (payable quarterly).

Proposition #10: Think Smart About Taxes

Most Canadians inadvertently reduce the returns from their investments by overpaying their taxes. They own too few equities and tax advantaged investments and own too many fixed income investments which generate only highly taxed interest income. Here are some steps to reduce your tax liability:

1. Capital gains can be earned tax-free in the name of children and grandchildren - up to $10,000 per year per child.

2. AGF, Canadian International, and GT Global are three mutual fund companies which issue special, deferred capital gains, mutual fund investments which everyone should at least investigate.

3. Dividend income is worth more to you than interest income because it is taxed at a significantly lower rate - so you keep more! Seek out stock plans which allow you to reinvest your dividends for free or at a discount.

Maximizing your RRSP contributions, using Labour Sponsored Investment Funds where appropriate, investing in mutual fund limited partnerships and seeking out quality oil & gas and real estate investments are the last, good quality, tax ameliorated investments in Canada.

WEALTH ODYSSEY - THE ULTIMATE PORTFOLIO

In this final part of our Wealth Odyssey to maximize wealth by doubling our net worth every five years, we can now create the optimal portfolio. This portfolio recognizes the ten propositions we have outlined in the first three sections of this series and answers the basic question: What assets should be held in what proportion?

Obviously, every Canadian needs their own customized financial plan based on a thorough understanding of their own personal needs, risk preference, income requirements, and family goals and objectives. This is the role of your expert advisor - your professional financial planner or broker.

To better understand this process, however, it may be necessary to review a sample proposed portfolio for an investor at, say, age fifty today. Based on an initial investment of $100,000 and additional investment income on an annual basis, this portfolio should be able to produce a net worth of almost $1 million in fifteen years at age sixty-five. Hence, a safe and secure retirement regardless of the economic threats we are, and will continue to be, confronted with.

Soft Assets - 80% of Net Worth

20%   "Great Business" stocks paying dividends (using our Top Ten List)

30%   Geographically diverse, value-oriented, mutual funds such as: Trimark, Ivy, AGF Canadian, Templeton, Universal Select, Fidelity Far East, 20/20 World Equity, AIC Value & Advantage, O'Donnell U.S. Mid-Cap

10%   Convertible "Triple B" Bonds

5%   Momentum Funds: Marathon, 20/20 Aggressive Growth, O'Donnell Emerging Market

10%   T-Bills, Cash, Money Market Funds

Hard Assets - 20% of Net Worth

10%   Oil & Gas development partnerships and Royal Trust Units

10%   Canadian real estate (for shelter and family security) U.S. real estate (for investment and tax considerations)

This portfolio should provide you with:

1. an average annual net yield of 16%-22%;

2. lower overall taxes by maximizing dividends, capital gains, and tax-free returns;

3. increased growth by constantly reinvesting your
    returns to magnify the compounding effect;

4. personal peace of mind and greater financial security
    by diversifying your portfolio on the basis of
    geography, financial product, market, and manage-
    ment expertise;

5. currency protection (some assets can be purchased
    in U.S. dollars to provide a currency hedge while
    other investments generate cash flow in U.S. dollars);

6. a clear and integrated multidimensional strategy.

So, where should we be at the end of this process?

Well, if you put $100,000 into a GIC or Canada
Savings Bond at current interest rates with reinvesting,
it would produce about $115,000 in five years, after
taxes and inflation.

In contrast, a $100,000 investment in our Wealth
Odyssey - The Ultimate Portfolio would reasonably be
expected to grow into $225,000 in five years, subject to
the same level of tax, inflation, and annual reinvestments.

The choice is yours; you be the judge.

INVESTING IN MUTUAL FUNDS IS COMPLEX

In 1997, Canadians have $208 billion invested in 1,340
different mutual funds. Believe it or not, in 1986, eleven
years ago, we had only $10 billion in mutual funds. But
the reason isn't hard to see. Of the 225 mutual funds

that have been around for longer than ten years in Canada, only one has lost money in absolute terms. This simple test means that most fund managers will produce for you.

However, given the sheer complexity of investing in 1996, we need to use a large number of criteria to assess whether any particular mutual fund is good for us. Here are some of the most important factors that you should consider and discuss with your financial advisor if you are considering a mutual fund investment.

The Prospectus: Every mutual fund, by law, has to have a prospectus and provide it to you. Make sure you get a copy and read it carefully. Understand exactly what you are investing in and why.

Performance: Look for a fund that has at least five years of performance. If you are looking to invest in a new fund, at least make sure that the lead manager has five years of above average performance in previous positions.

Also, ask your financial advisor to analyze the fund for the level of risk the fund manager takes in order to earn the returns he generates, and then compare the returns he generates and compare the returns and risk to other funds in the same category. Look for year-to-year con- sistency of performance. This means that you don't want "one year wonders" or "flavour of the month" funds. The most important issue is consistency of growth and returns over a long period of time.

Investment Philosophy: There are different types of investment strategies, and they do make a difference. Does your fund manager follow a value, momentum, "top-down," "bottom-up," market timing or sector rotation (to name just a few) investment philosophy? Value investors tend to produce the greatest long-term consistency of growth. Other questions you should ask relate to how (if at all) they hedge their funds and what kind of exposure do you have with these derivatives.

Portfolio Manager: Obviously, you should know the person making your investment decisions. Who is the manager? What is their background? As a rule of thumb, the longer they have been around, the more secure and consistent the returns they have been able to generate.

Some other factors are also important to understand and ask questions about. For example, there is the issue of size. Generally speaking, the larger the fund, the more consistent the returns. There is also the question of "turnover," which is the degree of frequency with which individual securities are bought or sold by the fund manager. One little understood fact is that the greater the turnover of your fund, the greater is the tax liability you have.

Finally, there are the cost and client service factors which very frequently are either completely ignored or misunderstood in terms of the impact they have on you as an investor. The expense ratio is a measure of cost which illustrates how efficiently the fund company manages its business. The higher the expense ratio, the lower the returns to the investor, especially in the bond and money markets where the expense ratio is the key criterion.

Finally, the level of service is a factor. Are you dealing with a stranger over the telephone who is simply taking orders without offering any good advice? Or are you dealing with a full-service advisor who really under-stands your needs and financial situation?

Remember, buying mutual funds can be a good invest-ment for financial returns. But tread carefully, educate yourself, know what questions to ask and what to look for.

OUR RESEARCH - TESTING NEW INVESTING STRATEGIES

Over the years, we are always coming across new approaches to investing that involve hybrid methods of beating markets and earning superior income. Almost all are targeted to the sophisticated investor with a computer and financial software that tracks the num-bers. Several do seem to work in the short term. Although we do not recommend these approaches to the average investor, here are a few of the newest in vogue ideas.

1. Buying the Top

We often scoff at people who buy the winning mutual fund of the previous year as "flavour of the month" investors, but are they wrong to do this?

Researchers set out to determine how you would do if you bought the top diversified equity mutual fund of the year just ended, held it one year, and then replaced it with the top performers for the subsequent year.

An investor who started with $1,000 and followed that strategy from 1975 to 1995 would have accumulated $78,108 for an average annual gain of 24.3%. The same investment in the average for diversified mutual funds would have grown to $15,534; a return of 14.7%. The winner from each year outperformed the average in the following year fifteen years out of twenty; one year was a tie.

Why does this strategy work? Because it is limited to U.S. diversified funds instead of volatile sector funds that jump up and down with things like gold prices or technology stocks. The stock market tends to move in cycles of three to five years, meaning that the winning fund's investing style often has another year or two of favour remaining. Only U.S. data is available on this concept.

2. The Dow Theory Applied to Mutual Funds

Dow Theory suggests that if we buy the top ten stocks with the highest yields that make up the thirty stocks in the Dow Jones Industrial Average each month or year and change our portfolio to replace them with the highest yields over the next period, we will outperform the market. The same method is being applied to mutual funds.

Researchers selected the top ten all-equity mutual funds at the end of each month, then replaced them with the next month's top ten list a program of trading in and out of each month's top ten list. The returns on this approach for the six months we have listed with U.S. data only has been 19% while the Dow average rose 10%.

Even better, the gains could be tax sheltered in full inside an RRSP. Commissions may not be high as many funds continue as monthly leaders; some are no-load and others may be a switch commission fee as they are in the same family of funds.

One caution: The Canadian market is less diversified and performs less well than the U.S. market over time. It is more cyclical and less likely to produce equivalent returns, but the concept is worthy of further analysis.

3. The Dow Dividend Theory

To create the portfolio, identify the top ten highest dividend yielding stocks (annual dividend divided by share prices) and buy equal amounts of each. A high dividend yield which moves inversely to price indicates an out-of-favour stock. Hold the shares for a year, not making a single trade for twelve months no matter what happens. At the end of the year, rebalance.

We continue to believe that value investing on a buy and hold basis is the best long-term option for equities and equity mutual funds.

INVESTMENT TIPS - AVOIDING MEDIOCRITY MUTUAL FUND DANGER SIGNS

Interestingly, when asked about their investments, most Canadians believe they do better than they actually do. In addition, when asked about mutual funds, almost all people will say that we are living in boom times.

Reality Check

The first attitude is called the "halo effect" (bad news happens to other people). The second attitude confuses asset accumulation (which is booming) and financial returns to investors (which varies widely). Unfortunately, both of these attitudes mask reality.

With over 1,100 different funds available in Canada, the strong performance and media exposure of the "blue chip" funds (for example, Templeton, AGF, Trimark, Fidelity, Mackenzie, etc.) often mask the relatively poor performance of the great majority of the smaller funds.

Research and experience has shown that four factors consistently conspire against even the most talented managers. Can you recognize a fund in trouble? What if it is one in which you have invested?

Danger signs?

Here are some danger signs to watch out for.

Ballooning Assets: Investing is much easier with $10 million or even $100 million in a fund than it is with $1 billion.

Blurred Vision: At best, this happens when fund managers are forced to broaden the scope of their search for appropriate investments. At worst, it is simply an unfocussed investment strategy.

Fund Pile Up: Because most fund companies stress the accumulation of assets as a major priority, pressure is constant to bring new funds to market. Pretty soon your manager is managing twice the number of funds (and spending half as much time managing each one).

Management Problems: More funds and more assets under administration mean more management headaches, the need for better technology, and the need for greater research capabilities (which may not always be available).

So what questions should you ask to ferret out problems in your fund portfolio?

- Has the fund company been the subject of negative publicity? How did the company respond?

- Did the advertising prove to be misleading once you reviewed the fund's investment strategy, fees, and past performance?

- Does the fund have inconsistent performance or invest in highly volatile securities such as restricted stocks, derivatives, high risk debt, illiquid mortgage related assets, or speculative trading practices involving futures, options, margin buying, or short selling?

- Does the fund have a rising ratio of expenses to assets under administration or a fee schedule which seems to be increasingly difficult to figure out?

- Is the fund's historical performance inconsistent (or worse, subpar) relative to the market in general or similar funds?

Bailing Out

The first thing is to always insure that you review your portfolio at least twice per year (and quarterly if you can). Also, review your fund company's annual reports and the prospectus. Also, be sure to speak candidly with your financial advisor about future prospects.

After you have done your research and discovered a problem, how do you know it is time to bail out? Never become emotionally attached to your investments. On the other hand, don't make a hasty decision. As even the best managers have off years, you are best advised to give your fund manager a maximum two years grace for poor performance, then pull the trigger.

TIME-OUT FOR MARKET TIMING

Given all the talk about the phenomenal returns in 1995 and an impending market correction, many people are talking about "market timing" as an investment strategy. However, we recently came across some interesting thoughts on this issue by Peter Lynch. Although he is no doubt too busy to provide us with his comments directly, we still felt it worthwhile to distill some of this great investor's thinking on the merits of market timing.

With all the research illustrating the superior long-term performance of equities over bonds and especially fixed income investments, why is it that the vast majority of Canadians are still hopelessly devoted to GICs, T-Bills, Canada Savings Bonds, and Money Market funds? It seems the only logical explanation is what Peter Lynch once called our irrational "fear of crashing." That somehow, even though equities unquestionably provide the best return, we are afraid that the moment we invest our own money, the market will suddenly, inexplicably turn against us and our hard-earned cash will go down the drain.

For those investors already in the market, now is the time they typically try to prepare for the impending downturn by hedging, "cashing out," or rebalancing their portfolios to reduce their equity exposure. The reality has been that far more money has been lost during previous corrections either by investors panicking and selling out at a loss or by timidly sitting on the sidelines while big profits are made during the recovery. Either way, investors lost out big time.

So what does Peter Lynch advise? Nothing.

First of all, a correction is coming; you can bet on it! When? Who cares? Lynch's point, however, is that market timing is largely irrelevant; it doesn't matter whether your timing is good or bad. Take the following example based on Lynch's research in the United States:

If you invested $2,000 in the S&P 500 Index on January 1 every year since 1965, your annual return would have been 11.0%. But, if you were lucky enough to invest that same $2,000 every year at the low point of the S&P 500 for that year, your annual return would have been 11.7%. However, if your timing stunk and you made that same investment at the peak of the market, you would still have managed a 10.6% return.

For most investors, this difference is largely irrelevant. Just in case you think Peter Lynch's calculator has broken, the Chicago financial consulting firm of Ibbotsen Associates drew similar conclusions. In their 1995 study, they compared the returns from a $10,000 investment at the peak of the stock market every year between 1979 and 1995 with the returns from an annual $10,000 investment in T-Bills that very same day. Their findings were that over that sixteen-year period, the stock market investment had grown to $540,000 while the T-Bill investment was worth slightly less than $280,000.

Lynch's lesson: Time, not timing, is the formula for success. Forget market timing; the point is to stay invested in stocks and don't panic when that inevitable downturn comes.

A Pantheon of Great Investors

Financial professionals consider these people among the greatest investors of all time. Even in this select group, Warren Buffet stands out.

Name	Main Affiliation	Estimated Returns (1)	Comments
Warren Buffet	Berkshire Hathaway	Up 27% a year since 1957	Wants to invest in "wonderful businesses." favourite holding period: forever.
Benjamin Graham	Graham-Newman	Up 17% a year, 1929-56	Considered the father of value investing. Liked stocks that are cheap relative to earning or book value.
John Maynard Keynes	National Mutual Life Assurance Society (Britain)	Up most year during treacherous 1930s markets	Famous economist was also an avid and serious investor. Posted big losses but even bigger gains.
Peter Lynch	Fidelity Magellan Fund	Up 29% a year, May 1977-May 1990	Bought dozens of stocks in industries he favoured. Workaholic until his surprise "retirement."

A Pantheon of Great Investors (continued)

Name	Main Affiliation	Estimated Returns (1)	Comments
Bob Kremball	Trimark	15.28 since 1981	Value investing long term.
George Soros	Quantum Fund	Up 34% a year since 1969	Huge bets on international currencies and bonds; uses major leverage.
Jonathon Wellum	AIC Value	23.5%	Great businesses: Warren Buffet style.
John Templeton	Templeton Growth Fund	Up 18% a year, November 1954-March 1987	Bargain hunter worldwide; a pioneer of international investing

BASIC GUIDELINES FOR INVESTING IN EMERGING MARKETS

Following the sharp drop in domestic interest rates in late 1993 and early 1994, many inexperienced investors, looking for higher and better returns, were lured into new investment markets such as Asia and Latin America for the first time. The lessons have been painful and losses to capital frightening.

Our three basic objectives in the 1990s against which all financial decisions are made are: preserving capital, reducing risk, and enhancing returns. If an investment does not meet these standards, it is usually inappropriate.

At no time were investments in Latin America, Asia, and Emerging Markets meant to be a replacement for fixed income investing such as bonds or mortgage-backed securities. Emerging Markets are highly volatile areas where value can rise or fall by a third or more over a twelve-month period.

Lesson #1 - The 5% Rule

Remember that Emerging Markets should be 5-10% of a portfolio for young aggressive investors and certainly no more than 5% for older conservative investors.

Yes, Canada holds only 2.8% of the world's equity markets, and international diversification with the U.S. and Western Europe is essential to reduce risk and enhance returns, but newer economies while offering huge potential gains are usually balanced by equally higher risk.

Emerging Markets dropped sharply in the spring and summer of 1994, and many are still struggling, especially Mexico. Others like Brazil and Hong Kong are doing well again, but for how long?

Lesson #2 - The 7% Rule

U.S. interest rates profoundly affect capital inflows and outflows in Emerging Markets. When U.S. rates drop, they encourage investors to invest abroad to get higher returns. Between 1990 and 1993, U.S.$150 billion flooded into Latin America, Mexico, Asia, and Eastern Europe. But when U.S. rates rose in 1994, the money flowed out just as quickly. In Mexico, this outflow was a fundamental cause of the financial crisis in December 1995.

In 1997, the cycle is repeating itself. Money is flowing back into Emerging Markets again, as U.S. interest rates fall. The basic rule is that as long as U.S. long-term rates are 7% or less, money will flow to Emerging Markets.

To prevent local disasters, many economies are limiting inflows of foreign cash. This is good for high savings economies such as Chile, Argentina, and Hong Kong.

The softest markets are the ones that are controlling liquidity, especially with the softening of the American economy. Interest rates are likely to continue to fall for months to come. Do not get caught in speculative bubbles. Follow the rates and remember the 7% rule.

EVALUATING INFRASTRUCTURE PROJECTS IN EMERGING MARKETS

Recently, infrastructure projects in Emerging Markets have been receiving a lot of press. If you are interested in investing companies in this line of work, here are some brief tips to minimize risks if you consider going this route:

Right Business:
Some businesses are more politically sensitive than others, and never, never underestimate the impact of local political issues on the success of foreign business ventures.

Financing Arrangements:
Past experience in Emerging Markets has shown that in a crisis, debt obligations are more likely to be honoured than equity obligations.

Local Partners:
A company is much more likely to be successful if it has partners or strong relationships with local companies or business leaders.

Innovative Agreements:
Ensure that projects protect the best interests of both the project and the host country and are flexible enough to grow and evolve over time.

Financial Protection:
A project or firm should obtain direct insurance and seek enforceable government guarantees to protect their interests.

Disputes:
Ensure any agreements include a sensible dispute resolution mechanism.

The Economic Cycle

Technology Transportation

1. Early Expansion

Duration: About 17 months
Inflation: Continuing to fall
Interest Rates: Bottoming out

Service & Capital Goods

1. Middle Expansion

Duration: About 17 months
Inflation: Bottoming out
Interest Rates: Rising modestly

**Financials/Utilities/
Consumer Cyclicals**

1. Late Contraction

Duration: About 6 months
Inflation: Flat to declining
Interest Rates: Falling

Basic Materials Energy

1. Late Expansion

Duration: About 17 months
Inflation: Rising - Beginning to concern
Interest Rates: Rising rapidly

Health & Consumer Staples

1. Early Contraction

Duration: About 6 months
Inflation: Rising less strongly
Interest Rates: Peaking

THE ECONOMIC CYCLE

Sector investing gets its power from the fact that up to sixty cents of every dollar's move in a stock's price comes from trends in the overall market, and from whether a sector is in or out of favour.

Interested investors can turn to the 100 or so sector funds available. The economic cycle is the main guide for the investments listed in the "Standard & Poor's Guide to Sector Investing." As economic expansion picks up, transportation stocks will thrive as more and more goods are delivered. As demand continues to rise, companies seek to improve productivity through technology, so computer and other high-tech stocks also prosper.

As the economy reaches the middle phase of expansion, service stocks, like providers of temporary workers, rise as companies struggle to meet increased demand but remain reluctant to add to permanent overhead costs.

Finally, when the expansion is in full throttle, companies hire a few more workers but spend more money on capital goods. That makes stocks in machine tools, energy, and basic materials like steel the way to go. Then, and now, the contraction begins.

Sector investing is not for everyone. A sector investor must stay alert to economic developments and be able to tolerate above-average volatility. And watch out if you are chasing today's hot sector. On five of the seven occasions since 1985 when a sector was hot, many more investor dollars poured into funds after the sector delivered its best returns than before, according to a study by Morningstar, the mutual fund research company.

Moreover, remember that all investing models cannot fit all of the facts. The model, for example, does not explain the remarkable performance of high-tech stocks. And it assumes that future economic performance will reflect past economic performance. But a few economists say that the economy is changing so quickly that the future isn't what it used to be.

INVESTMENT TIPS - GLOBAL INVESTING: IT NEED NOT BE A MAD, MAD WORLD

Have you been thinking recently about "going global?" If you are less than enthused, you're not alone. After all, with all the potential pitfalls, why bother? Who hasn't heard the horror stories - revolutions, lax (or nonexistent) securities laws, wild currency gyrations, management fraud, and just plain old rude treatment, all of which can put your hard earned money at risk!

Why bother? Because you really have no choice. Consider this: Canadian stock markets collectively represent approximately 2% of total global stock market capitalization at present (which, unbelievably, is down from 4% in 1980). When it comes to your investment options, does it make sense for you to ignore 98% of the world's equity markets? Not in our opinion.

It is surprising how timid most Canadians are when it comes to global investing. According to the U.S. based Investment Company Institute, by the start of 1996, Americans had plunked $148.1 billion into international mutual funds. This is up from roughly $2.5 billion in 1985! Even applying the usual 10:1 ratio for comparing

Canadian and U.S. statistics, Canadians lag way behind. Ninety percent of Canadian investors have no exposure at all to investments outside of North America.

The reason you have no choice can be summed up in two words: diversification and growth.

In fact, our research has shown that the optimal equity investment structure to efficiently balance superior returns with minimum risk for any investor with a significant portfolio is 60% of assets in Canadian securities and 40% in international equities (see Efficient Frontier Graph below). So, if you don't want to be left out, here's a brief lesson on global investing: how to develop a strategy, identify opportunities, and avoid pitfalls.

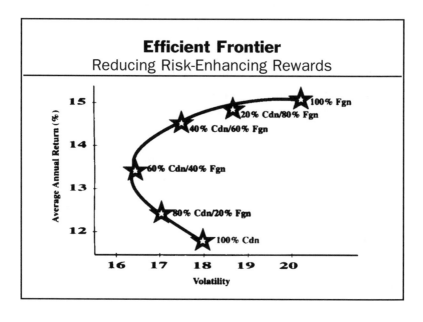

Global Firms

I have often heard it said that the best and least risky way to diversify internationally is to invest in blue chip Canadian firms which have a significant volume of international business. Although I can't dispute that this does provide some exposure to international markets, it overestimates the impact. Past research has shown that the stocks of Canadian internationals are much more heavily influenced by the ups and downs of the Canadian stock market, economy, and political developments than international business opportunities they pursue. This is because the majority of shares are generally held by Canadians whose investment decisions are heavily influenced by developments in Canada. This situation can be illustrated by the fact that even stocks in different countries, but in the same industry, follow their own stock market movement more closely than they follow each other.

Open End Mutual Funds

If the best globally diversified Canadian firms aren't going to do it for you, the next best option for most investors is your basic vanilla flavoured global mutual fund. It is the most efficient option and offers the best protection against excessive risk. These funds have a variety of investment objectives, ranging from broadly diversified global funds through index, region, and country funds to highly focussed "industry specific" funds (i.e., telecommunications or infrastructure).

99

Closed End Mutual Funds

In the pursuit of ever higher returns, "closed out" funds are your next option, but they carry significantly greater risk. Similar to more common and more numerous "open end" funds, these products pool investor funds for a specific objective, but that's as far as the parallel goes. These funds issue a fixed number of shares which then trade on an exchange like any other stock. This gives closed end funds a unique positioning which can be important to global investors.

On the positive side, closed funds are typically much smaller in size and more nimble in following opportunities. Management is also not committed to keeping a cash reserve on hand to fund redemptions, which means that the fund can remain fully invested at all times. The closed feature also provides a measure of protection from investor panic.

However, most important, is the fact that because the fund trades like any stock, investor sentiment can swing the price higher (to a premium) or lower (to a discount) relative to the net asset value of the fund itself. This "multiplier effect" accentuates the volatility of these international funds.

Foreign Stocks

There are two ways to invest directly in foreign stocks. The most common approach to this type of "do-it-yourself diversification" is to purchase shares of foreign companies which are listed on either the Toronto

Investing Overseas Diversifies Risk

Since overseas markets move differently from the S&P 500, they offset one another in portfolio.	Britain	0.55
	Canada	0.46
	France	0.43
	Australia	0.42
	Germany	0.33
Perfect correlation with the U.S. market = 1.00*	Hong Kong	0.31
	Indonesia	0.24
	Mexico	0.19
* Correlations based on monthly returns since 1991.	India	0.15
	Japan	0.14

Source: Fortune, September 30, 1996

Stock Exchange or the New York Stock Exchange. However, the greater risk in this approach is a direct result of buying individual shares of specific companies. To achieve the same type of diversification that a global mutual fund offers, you generally have to commit at least $100,000 - a hefty admission fee. Nevertheless, as more foreign companies look to North America to raise money, this option is becoming increasingly common. For example, in a recent speech to the National Investors Relations Institute in Naples, Florida, the income president of the NYSE, William Johnson, stated that over the next ten years, he expects the number of foreign firms listed on the NYSE will grow from roughly 250 to 700.

For those of you who sleep very soundly, shares can be purchased in foreign companies that are listed only on their home exchange, anywhere from Argentina to Zimbabwe. Needless to say, the risks can knock your socks off, but conversely, the potential returns (if you pick 'em right) can be awesome.

So, if you have no choice but to go global, are there any useful tips we can pass on to keep your hair from falling out? Try these:

1. In global investing, even more than here at home, the reputation, experience, and track record of your money manager is paramount.

2. Make sure your mutual fund is doing what it is supposed to do. Understand its stated objectives (as outlined in the prospectus) and make sure the investment allocation matches it. (The flight from Mexico in 1994 during its currency crisis suggests that many funds had overweighted Mexican investments.)

3. Make sure you know how much fund money is actually going into stocks. Remember, global investing involves investments denominated in foreign currencies. It is possible for mutual funds to "hedge" their currency risk by buying currency futures contracts to lock in an exchange rate. While some funds don't hedge at all, others may hedge up to 50% of their investments. This means that up to 50% of the assets in the fund are tied up in currency hedges rather than in equity investments. Surprise!

4. Obtain the assistance of a professional financial

advisor who can evaluate your financial needs, investment objectives, and risk sensitivity to develop a reasonable and properly weighted portfolio of global investments for you (see three sample portfolios following).

5. Have a "buy" strategy. If you are going global by reallocating existing investments into foreign content, develop a systematic plan to transfer assets over two or three years (for example, a preset amount like $1,000 per month or a gradual asset sale which would minimize taxable income and capital gains considerations). In contrast, if you are investing "new" money, past research has proven that "lump sum investing" (regardless of the timing) generates superior returns to a "dollar cost averaging" approach.

6. Be prepared to spend some time educating yourself. Take some responsibility for understanding the international financial marketplace and the way foreign political, economic, and financial developments can affect your investments.

   For those of you who are already heeding this advice, "surfing the Internet" is perhaps the information source of the future in this regard. Here are some of the best online sources of information for international investing as selected by the staff of the Wall Street Journal:

Surf's Up

ASIAN BUSINESS WATCH
http://www.webcom.com/darrel/

BARRA EMERGING MARKETS VOLATILITY INDEX
http://www.barra.com/MarketInfo/emvi.html

BLOOMBERG NEWS SERVICE
http://www.bloomberg.com

CHINA NEWS DIGEST
http://cnd.end.org/

CURRENCY RATES
http://www.yahoo.com/Economy/Markets-and-Investments/Currency Exchange/

FINANCIAL TIMES OF LONDON (FT.COM)
http://www.ft.com/

INTERNET CORRUPTION RANKING
http://www.gwdg.de/-uwyw/icr.htm/
KNIGHT-RIDDER FINANCIAL NEWS
http://www.cnnfn.com/news/knight_ridder/

THE OFFSHORE ENTREPRENEUR
http://www.au.com/offshore/sample/
THE WALL STREET JOURNAL INTERACTIVE EDITION
http://wsj.com

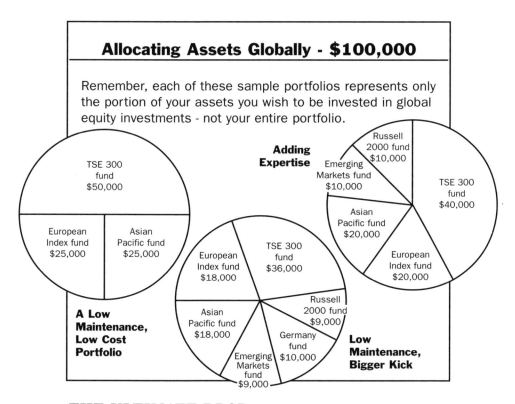

Allocating Assets Globally - $100,000

Remember, each of these sample portfolios represents only the portion of your assets you wish to be invested in global equity investments - not your entire portfolio.

A Low Maintenance, Low Cost Portfolio

TSE 300 fund $50,000
European Index fund $25,000
Asian Pacific fund $25,000

Adding Expertise

Russell 2000 fund $10,000
Emerging Markets fund $10,000
Asian Pacific fund $20,000
TSE 300 fund $40,000
European Index fund $20,000

Low Maintenance, Bigger Kick

TSE 300 fund $36,000
European Index fund $18,000
Asian Pacific fund $18,000
Emerging Markets fund $9,000
Germany fund $10,000
Russell 2000 fund $9,000

THE ULTIMATE RRSP

Should you make your RRSP decisions on the basis of what is ideal just for 1997 or best for you over the long term? The answer is particularly clear in light of the 2.5% GIC rates and the performance of major equity markets. We must always make RRSP decisions as long-term retirement planning vehicles and not as short-term portfolio decisions.

Most investors choose what they consider to be the safest bets for their RRSP. Buying a GIC was always synonymous with investing in an RRSP. Obviously, the interest income accrued tax free in the body of the RRSP.

As interest rates fell in 1995, strip bonds were useful as they produced excellent capital gains that could be tax-deferred inside an RRSP. But neither of these options offer the long-term growth needed by Canadians for their RRSP investing.

The RRSP is in some ways like any other investment portfolio. But with properly structured foreign content and the ability to defer tax liability to retirement, the returns with proper asset allocation can obviously be dramatically greater, especially because of our ability to reinvest inside the RRSP and compound at a greater rate of return.

Each age category requires an RRSP structure that is both long term in strategy and partially reflective of current market conditions. We can achieve both objectives, especially if we understand that your RRSP is not a short-term depository from which we can regularly withdraw cash. The loss of the compounding power of the money in the RRSP when withdrawn is next to impossible to make up.

At least 70% of the money inside your RRSP should be put away into longer term investments (five to ten years) and essentially treated as "forgotten holdings." The other 30% should reflect the best one to three year market conditions.

Here are some sample RRSP portfolios we now call "age optimal RRSP bundles."

Young - growing income - at least thirty years or more to retirement

(Use special mutual funds with high foreign content that count as Canadian and even small business shares to take foreign content level to 36% or more):

25% - Equities (dividend or preferred shares)
45% - Equity Mutual Funds (Canada, U.S., Europe)
10% - Emerging Markets & Small Cap Equity funds
20% - Government of Canada Strip Bonds (twenty, thirty, forty years)

Middle Aged, Middle Income - less than twenty years to retirement

20% - Blue Chip Equities (Canada, U.S., Europe, Japan)
20% - Equity Mutual Funds (Canada, U.S., Europe)
15% - Balanced Mutual Funds (Canadian)
10% - Government of Canada ten to twenty year strip bonds
10% - Growth & Income Mutual Funds (Canadian)
10% - CMIIC Mortgage Backed Securities
10% - Five-Year Alberta/B.C. Government Bonds
 5% - Emerging Market Funds

Older, Mature Preretirement - ten years or less to invest

15% - Blue Chip Equities (Canada, U.S.)
15% - Major Market Equity Funds
20% - Balanced Mutual Funds (Canadian)
30% - Five-Year and Ten-Year Provincial Bonds
(Alberta, B.C.) and Ten-Year Government of Canada
Bonds

10% - Mortgage Backed Securities
10% - GICs

Try to acquire bonds and mortgages and GICs with staggered maturity dates with 10%-20% of your holdings maturing each year.

Be sure to maximize foreign content. All portfolios, regardless of the age of the investor, should include about 10% in resource industries, particularly oil & gas shares, royalty trust units, and liquid Canadian qualifying energy securities.

It is this type of structure that reduces risk, preserves capital, and dramatically enhances returns in the body of your RRSP.

WHY YOU MUST USE ASSET ALLOCATION

Since 1991, research has proven that the basic decision about how your portfolio is divided between equities, bonds, and cash determines 91% of your financial performance. Asset allocation as it is called is an essential tool to reduce risk and enhance returns. Too few Canadians have an asset allocation plan that is customized to their age, income, risk tolerance, and goals and objectives.

In fact, most Canadians have little asset allocation at all. Their portfolio consists primarily of cash-related investments like Canada Savings Bonds, T-Bills, and GICs, along with nonperforming real estate. Every investor needs to craft a custom model that is flexible according to their own circumstances, age, income, and view of the market.

We have prepared a planning model for asset allocation using current available taxable income. You can complete it and customize it to your situation. The model works backwards from your equity allocation to determine how much in bonds and cash you need.

Step One

Step One of this model helps you set your ideal allocation of stocks and stock funds based on the following criteria:

Age: Since young people can afford to take more risk, score ten points if you're over forty or under, zero points if you're sixty or over.

Net Worth: The more you have, the less risk you need to take. Score seven points if you have less than $200,000 and five if you have between $200,000 and $1 million.

Income: This is the inverse of net worth. The more income you have, the more risk you can afford. Score five points for less than $100,000 and ten for more than $250,000.

Risk Tolerance: This one's up to you. Can you afford to let your investments sit for at least five years? Can you be productive at work when your stocks are down? Score ten for a high risk tolerance, zero for an extremely low tolerance of risk.

Optimism: This is how you feel about the economy and

the stock market, not your own personal optimism. The more optimistic you feel about the market, the more you will be putting into stocks.

After you've filled in your optimism score, tally up your total. Then multiply by two to get your equity allocation. If you scored thirty-two, for example, your equity allocation would be 64%.

Step Two

Step Two of the worksheet helps you divide your remaining funds between bonds and cash (or cash equivalents such as GICs, money market funds, and savings bonds). Answer the same questions again, but don't simply put down your score for Step One. Some of the scoring is different for Step Two. For instance, you may want to register a different confidence level for the bond market than you did for stocks. We would score a six here. Inflation remains low, but bonds won't likely have as good a year in 1997 as they did in 1995.

Let's say you scored a thirty-seven in Step Two of the worksheet. Multiplied by two, your bond score is 74%, which means that 74% of the money you're not putting into stocks should be invested in bonds. The rest of your assets should be invested in cash or cash equivalents.

Step Three

Step Three of the worksheet helps you translate those last two allocations into a fixed percentage of your total funds. Remember, you already have 64% of your total funds in stocks. Thus, the 74% of your fixed income funds going into bonds would be 26.64% of your total funds (74% of 36%, or 0.74 x 0.36). Similarly, the cash portion would be 9.36% of your total funds (26% of 36%, or 0.26 x 0.36).

Investment Planning

"I used to be a financial advisor on Wall Street. I used to manage other people's money until it was all gone!"

- Woody Allen

The rich do in fact have investment plans of a long-term nature. Rarely do they buy things at random without a plan. If you look at a *Fortune* or *Forbes* listing of the 100 richest people in the world, not one is a stock picker, market timer, or sector rotator. Nor are they concerned about the short term, market psychology, or political events. They tend with few exceptions to be long-term buy and hold investors. They look for business equities in mutual funds (72% hold them) or as individual equities.

They realize they will need growth at least until age seventy-five. They know they can't rely on the government for their retirement.

There are regional differences. While there is general acceptance of asset allocation and diversification, Western Canadians assume more risk and want higher returns than those in the East. Women take on less equities but still carry diversified portfolios.

Asset allocation is critical. It explains 91% of the variance in a portfolio's performance. This way you are allocated between equities, bonds, and cash. The soft assets are critical to reduce risk, enhance returns, and preserve capital. International diversification appears even more critical. The rich seem to recognize that Canada represents only 3% of the world equity market and there is a need to take advantage of what the world has to offer.

To enforce this, our research found that the average foreign content of the middle class who hold equities was less than 7%. The point of maximum volatility — fluctuations year to year of lowest return — was at 100% Canadian content.

This is the classic middle market investor. They hold GICs, Canada Savings Bonds, and daily interest savings accounts and local real estate. The optimal position for long-term asset preservation and highest return with lowest volatility was 60% Canadian content and 40% foreign investments. The rich were at about 36% foreign content, or close to optimal threshold.

The rich rarely use banks for financial advice (10%) but tend to use brokers or financial planners (65%) for advice and assistance.

Everyone seems to need a proper investment plan in the context of the total financial plan. We must view all the consequences of our actions.

Every time we make an investment we consume cash, create an asset that must be protected, create retirement income consequences, make it part of our estate and generate tax consequences. Nothing is in isolation. Every decision on investing seems to have at least five consequences and interactions.

Another factor consistent with the rich is the movement out of traditional real estate and into financial assets. While 98% own a home, they do so for accommodation purposes not as a primary investment.

The rich accept that they need about 80% in soft assets and 20% in hard asset-backed holdings. They invest in international real estate limited partnerships, oil and gas development partnerships, and other innovative holdings. They are now shying away from tax driven deals such as film and software limited partnerships because they rarely return capital and have poor returns.

The rich tend to read multiple sources of information on investing such as newsletters, prospectuses, and books and tend to be more computer literate. They are aggressive information seekers who understand that decisions cannot be made in isolation without good backup and background information.

The cornerstones are:

1. Think long term
2. Buy and hold investing
3. Asset allocation
4. Go heavy on equities
5. Asset growth until age seventy-five
6. International diversification
7. 80% soft assets/20% hard assets
8. Investing based on knowledge

Other rules of thumb to follow include:
1. The 7% rule: If U.S. interest rates (short term) are under 7%, money rushes out to emerging markets, Latin America, and Southeast Asia to yield higher returns. If

interest rates are above 7%, money rushes out of these markets back into the U.S. to have 7%+ with certainty and no risk, causing these markets to drop sharply.

2. The 100 yen (Japan) to the U.S. dollar rule: When there are less than 100 yen to the dollar (like 91 in the spring of 1996), the Japanese market falls because exports are too expensive. If the yen is over 100, it restores balance and the Japanese market does better.

3. The higher the foreign content the higher the return in the portfolio. At 100% foreign content your portfolio would be higher risk but would be at the highest yield point. At 60% Canadian it is at the lowest risk threshold.

4.. The minimum equity level in the portfolio should be 25% regardless of age.

5. The safest havens are the U.S., Western Europe, and Canada.

6. In every period from 1860 to date equities have outperformed fixed income investing in the U.S.

NOW DO IT!

When you start to create a proper investment strate-gy, your *first step* is to find out how comfortable you are, psychologically, with different levels of risk. This self-assessment, typically referred to as a "risk tolerance profile," plays a key role in developing a personal investment strategy by helping you understand how much risk you can live with without losing sleep at night and worrying yourself to death.

Your **second step** should be to determine how much risk you can absorb financially. This involves calculating the debt level you can service based on your current income and expenses. This calculation will illustrate, based on reasonable assumptions, how much leverage would be appropriate for investment purposes, how much interest payments on the debt would be, and whether you can afford the expense without undue financial hardship.

Once you have completed these first two steps, then you must make some ***basic investment decisions;*** for example, "What investments should I purchase?" and "How much of each different investment should I purchase?" The best way to do this is, with the assistance of your professional financial advisor, to create a simple model asset allocation. Now you are ready to make some basic decisions.

To sum up, we discovered in our research that most of the successful investors we interviewed told us that they do have an overall investment strategy. These individuals do not make isolated financial decisions; rather, they have a clear vision of what they are trying to do. It is like a jigsaw puzzle in which the picture is the overall investment strategy and each piece of the puzzle is a financial decision. Each decision is different, but they all fit together. People will obviously have different objectives as a result of unique personal situations, and different strategies to reach their objectives, but the research shows that there are some common elements: owning a home, maintaining a high proportion of their investments in equities, using computers and financial software to help them make decisions, using reasonable leverage, diversifying their portfolio internationally, maximizing RRSP contributions, and insuring that their financial plan is monitored and updated regularly.

THE STREETS ARE PAVED WITH GOLD

For some strange reason Canadians wish to hear negative things about Canada and investing in this country. Yet as I have said repeatedly in seminars across Canada, the *"streets are paved with gold"* here and our problem has become that we have gotten a little too lazy to bend over and pick it up.

We have investment opportunities that Americans would love to have but do not. We have some of the best investment options with the lowest risk and highest returns, and we have a surprisingly generous income tax act, which if properly followed permits good planning options.

Here are just a few of these golden options:

1. Income Splitting: We can set up investments to earn capital gains in the hands of children, grandchildren, nieces, and nephews (under eighteen) in trust that can avoid any attribu tion, and the first $10,000 a year of the capital gains will be tax free in the hands of the child.

2. We have Registered Education Savings Plans that let us accrue the income on $1,500 a year contributed to the plan for twenty-one years ($31,500) tax free, and then the child can take it out largely tax free to pay for education.

3. We have mutual funds that permit us to defer capital gains as long as we want, no matter how much we earn. This includes AGF International, G.T. Global Corporate, and C.I. Sector funds. It is like having a second RRSP to accrue capital gains tax free.

4. We are allowed 20% foreign content in RRSPs. There are, however, mutual funds considered Canadian content that are 20% foreign or more, taking the foreign content to 36% in our RRSP.

5. Our principal residence is not subject to a capital gains tax, but we can borrow against it for investment, making the interest cost tax deductible. We can also use part of the house for a home business, making household costs tax deductible against the income.

6. We can contribute charitable donations to museums, hospitals, art galleries, and universities, and the contribution will be 100%

tax deductible and not subject to the 20% of income-rule for charitable gifts.

7. We have long-term buy and hold investments such as Trimark (15.2% since 1982), Templeton Growth (15.1% over forty years), and the AIC Advantage Fund (23.5% since inception) with annual rates of return with a regularity that ensures you can double your net worth every five years by simply buying them and doing nothing.

8. We have investments like NCE Resources oil and gas development partnerships that permit a 100% tax write-off, a 21% rate of return payable quarterly, that can be 100% financed and produce a substantial capital gains when sold.

9. We have balanced funds for fixed income investors that pay 12% (Trimark Balance, AGF Balanced, Dynamic Partners), which is nearly triple the rate of a GIC.

10. We have section 153.(1.1) of the Income Tax Act where we can file as a Canadian Hardship Case. Use this to reduce your tax liability to get your taxes back in reduced quarterly installments or withholding tax at source today, not in a year when you file your return.

Is there any doubt that Canada is the greatest country in the world and that the *"streets are paved with gold?"*

THE WARREN BUFFET WAY

Value "Buy & Hold" Investing

Over the last forty years, we have seen some dramatic new evidence as to the effectiveness of various investment strategies. Two individuals have shed new light on investment success. These individuals are both investment visionaries: Sir John Templeton and Warren Buffet.

The concept of value investing is not new. It goes back to the 1950s and the writings of Benjamin Graham. The idea is to identify businesses that have unique market position, then purchase and hold their shares for a long period of time. This does not mean buying stocks or earnings; it does not mean buying trends, economic news, and market fluctuations; it does not mean being a stock picker, sector rotator, or market timer; it does mean investing in well-run businesses.

Warren Buffet has become America's most successful investor over the past thirty years. His company, Berkshire Hathaway, has become an immense entity making him America's second richest person after Bill Gates of Microsoft with a personal net worth of over $12 billion U.S., all from investing in businesses such as Coca-Cola, Gillette, American Express, and Capital Cities/ABC Broadcasting.

Sir John Templeton has had similar success with the Templeton Growth Fund. Since 1954, he has outperformed the market thirty-four out of the past forty years, producing an average annual rate of return of 15.2%.

Another "Warren Buffet Way" style company is Trimark, a company that has had incredible results for over a decade. The assets in their mutual fund portfolio have become one of the largest in Canada because of the rush to "quality and consistency." Their returns have consistently exceeded 15% and are based on value, "buy and hold" strategies. Bob Kremball, Trimark's guiding force, has made many Canadians very wealthy. Trimark and Templeton are both superb investments and are appropriate for any Canadian investor regardless of age.

A third and equally outstanding success that is not well known is the AIC Groups of Funds. Two of their products, the Advantage Fund and the Value Fund, are as pure Warren Buffet as you can get.

The AIC Advantage Fund is based on the premise that financial services companies are the growth and value industry of the '90s. The Advantage Fund buys shares of the major financial management companies such as Trimark, AGF, and Canadian International. AIC has been able to earn 18% returns because they capitalized on the growth of the industry by owning the publicly traded shares of these dynamic firms. Trimark shares came out on the Toronto Exchange at $12 in 1992 and now are up 535%. The Advantage Fund is a mutual fund of mutual fund company shares.

On the other hand, the AIC Value Fund owns shares in Berkshire Hathaway and the companies that Buffet himself invests in. An average of 18% annual return over five years is their norm, once again.

Buying businesses of unique value is the "Warren Buffet Way." These are three Canadian funds that have done a great job doing it his way.

When we compare the three most common investment strategies, "buy and hold," "market timing," and
"stock picking" over the last ten, twenty, and thirty
years, buy and hold always wins. It's the "Warren Buffet
Way" and the right way.

*"The first rule is not to lose: The second rule is
not to forget the first rule."*

- Warren Buffet

COMMODITIES — DON'T BUY GOLD!!!

When I first began to warn people about buying gold
in 1979, it was $960 Canadian an ounce and about to
collapse. There were long lines of lemmings (investors)
standing in front of the Bank of Nova Scotia and, of
course, this meant the speculative bubble was about to
burst. It did, and gold fell to $400 Canadian an ounce.

About five years ago, I again warned people about it.
Since then, it has risen $30 an ounce, a total of 10%
over five years. A poor investment at best.

Armageddonists warn us that in times of world strife
or inflation, gold prices soar. Well they haven't, and
often they don't. Only speculators make prices move.

Market demand has risen rapidly for gold in Southeast
Asia as these economies grow. While production is
dropping in Russia, it is up in South Africa and Australia
only marginally. In Canada, we are actually selling off all
our gold reserves. So what? Gold rose 8% to reflect the
real increase in demand. No other factors are relevant.

First of all, there is little inflationary pressure that the central banks won't stomp on the moment it exceeds 3%. In Canada, inflation might go as high as 1.7% this year and 2% next year, and in Toronto, it is 0 and likely to stay in that range.

Secondly, as for world strife, peace is breaking out all over the place, in the Middle East, Ireland, and Korea.

As an investment, gold has been one of the worst, only to be beaten out by silver. If we look at the U.S.-based figures over the last twenty years, we find that stocks grew at 13.1%, bonds at 10.2%, housing at 6.3%, inflation at 5.7%, gold at 4.5% and silver at 1%.

Even if we follow the last business cycle, the post-Gulf War recovery started at the beginning of 1992, gold prices fell to $330 then rose in July 1993 to $410. When the economy heated up and inflation fears and interest rates took off, it fell back to $370. The pattern is always the same. Gold prices rise rapidly at the beginning of the upturn, but as the economy takes off and inflation starts to increase gold falls as rates rise.

I really like gold for jewellery, watches, and even teeth but not as an investment. It is speculative and a poor performer. I like blue chip gold stocks, but not speculative listings in Vancouver or even the TSE. If desperate, I would even consider gold-based mutual funds that trade heavily in gold shares. But gold as a commodity is only for fools.

At least four times a year since 1979, I read these great prognostications of doom that hype the importance of buying gold now. I have ignored them for fifteen years and have been right. You do the same.

OFFSHORE ASSETS

Only about 28% of RRSP investors diversify internationally, and only 10% of all Canadian households have international or offshore holdings, principally in the United States.

While international diversification enhances returns in your RRSP, holding offshore assets can create some unusual tax liabilities for Canadians. Enhanced foreign content rules for RRSPs have allowed Canadians to hold up to 20% in foreign equities, mutual funds, or bonds. Strategic RRSP investors can, in fact, acquire Canadians mutual funds that hold up to 20% foreign content and increase RRSP yields by as much as 50% based on historical performance. This means going from a 10% tax-free yield to 15% and a legal 36% foreign RRSP content.

One can also purchase foreign currency, denominated Canadian bonds, and certain foreign market bonds as part of this foreign content rule. There are no negative implications for this strategy upon the death of the RRSP holder, especially if the plan has a spousal beneficiary permitting a tax-free rollover.

However, if you and your spouse hold foreign investments outside of your RRSP, such as U.S. stocks and bonds or U.S. real estate, a different tax liability scenario applies despite the Canada/U.S. Tax Treaty that gives you Canadian credits for U.S. taxes paid. Even if you hold your U.S. security investments in Canada, they are subject to U.S. taxes on dividends, gains, or income, and a U.S. tax filing is required.

How much is too much?

How many equity mutual funds should people hold of the same investment type before the benefits of diversification diminish? The figures below show the average statistical correlation between the number of funds in your portfolio and an underlying benchmark index. The higher the number, the greater the likelihood you'll mimic the market.

Number of funds in your portfolio	Growth	Growth & Income	Balanced	International
1	.91	.94	.91	.82
2	.93	.96	.95	.91
4	.95	.97	.96	.92
6	.95	.98	.96	.92
8	.95	.98	.97	.92
10	.99	.98	.97	.92

Data Prudential Diversified Investment Strategies

The most complex issue, however, is the implication of these assets as part of your estate. Canada and the U.S. have finally signed an accord on tax protocol on this matter. It is law as it has been ratified by the U.S. Congress and Canadian Parliament.

Up to the present time, U.S. estate taxes which can be as high as 55% of the value of the U.S. estate over $3 million did not quality for a tax credit for Canadians against "deemed disposition on death" capital gains taxes.

This new agreement provides for full tax credit on U.S. estate taxes paid by Canadians, a $1.2 million U.S. securities estate tax exemption, full refunds of estate taxes paid by Canadians from November 1988 to date, and an increased real estate credit rising from $60,000 U.S. to a prorated share of the $600,000 U.S. real estate credit based on the percentage of world income and assets in the United States.

This is an enormous gain for Canadians with U.S. assets and avoids the double taxation of the estate.

You should also be aware that after January 1996 if you retire to the U.S. or spend more than 183days a year there and you are receiving CPP or OAS payments, they will be subject to a 25% withholding tax by the federal government.

Despite these changes it is still advisable to consider holding U.S. assets jointly with your spouse. It avoids the taxes until the spouse's death and permits the doubling up of the estate tax exemptions and credits. Consider also selling U.S. assets well before and having insurance in place to pay any estate taxes. Trusts can also be useful here as well.

If your international assets are outside of North America, ask Revenue Canada if a tax treaty exists between Canada and the country of domicile of your foreign holdings and whether there are tax credits or exemptions. It is imperative to tax plan now.

International investing is a good method of diversification to reduce risk and enhance returns. Be sure to consider the estate planning implications of this as well.

THE GRAHAM-HARVEY TEST

The Holy Grail for any investor is to be able to accurately predict future returns of their mutual fund investments or equity portfolios. Based on some very interesting new research, Canadians may be a little closer to achieving this goal.

Typically, most Canadians make investment decisions by picking up a copy of the daily newspaper and reviewing the latest number in recent stock tables or mutual fund performance data. Those stocks or funds which have the best current performance usually get their money. Unfortunately, the problem with this "gross return" method is that it is nothing more than a record of past performance — it tells us very little about possible future returns.

An alternate method of evaluating equity performance is a "risk-return analysis." This technique, often used by financial magazines such as *Forbes* to rate and rank performance, tries to compare the gross returns a fund or stock portfolio generates with its associated risk. It does this by evaluating performance in both bull and bear markets to monitor its overall volatility. The benefit of this approach is that it recognizes that risk is an integral part of any investment. However, this method still fails to explain how risk is identified and whether performance is more a matter of pure luck or real expertise on the part of the fund manager.

For sophisticated investors, the most effective method until now has been the "Sharpe Ratio" which was developed by William Sharpe, a Nobel Price winning economist from Stanford University. This ratio is a calculation which compares a fund manager's success in beating "zero-risk" Treasury Bills with the amount of leverage he uses and the price volatility of the securities they invest in. Although it is a well-recognized measure, once again this ratio is lacking in that it offers no assessment of whether the level of risk is appropriate relative to actual returns generated.

To rectify this deficiency, two American business school professors have recently presented new research into an improved risk/return performance model. Briefly, the model works by initially profiling a manager's fund in terms of diversification and leverage. Based on this profile, the next step is to create a hypothetical index fund with equivalent diversification and leverage. This allows an investor to measure both the actual returns and the volatility (i.e., risk) incurred by the fund against an appropriate benchmark.

From this exercise, any investor can evaluate not only actual performance but also the relative volatility (i.e., level of risk) the manager took to generate their returns. If the manager took significantly more risk than the index fund without achieving proportionately greater returns, he is underperforming the market and the fund likely will not generate superior returns over the long run. In contrast, if the investor's portfolio achieves equivalent returns with significantly less risk, the manager is outperforming the market.

Subsequent evaluation supported this finding — the Graham-Harvey test was twice as accurate in relating early and later performance of the same fund as the Sharpe Ratio.

Further details on this research can be found in Working Paper No. 4890, published by the National Bureau of Economic Research in Cambridge, Massachusetts.

CLASSIC RRSP MISTAKES

The fact that only 52% of adult Canadians who qualify for an RRSP have actually invested in one, highlights the obvious: Most RRSP holders have less than $31,000, yet will need at least $500,000 to ensure a retirement income of $25,000 a year.

Mistakes are everywhere. We rarely, if ever, contribute the maximum permissible amount and assume just because we can carry forward the uncontributed allowance seven years, we will someday make it up.

But by not contributing as much as possible, we forego the tax-free earnings that would add tens of thousands of dollars to our RRSPs. We then proceed to wait until year end or March 1 of the next year to contribute. By acting early each year, we can add $100,000 to the value of an RRSP. The average gain is 10% or more to the RRSP if the contribution is made *at the start* of the tax year, not the end.

Few of us have used our $8,000 over-contribution allowance that, while not producing a deduction, can accrue earnings tax free in the RRSP — adding an additional 7-10% to the long-term value of the RRSP.

Some of us view the RRSP as a short-term resting place for money; a place to create a tax deduction for this year and then as a source for cash withdrawals like a bank account. RRSP money should be treated as conservative retirement money that must be held essentially to retirement and drawn upon only as a last resort.

We constantly avoid setting up spousal plans as if one retirement income will be enough. We deny the existence of government clawbacks and the loss of age credits, yet clearly the only way to reduce taxes on retirement is for each spouse to have an income stream and separate plan.

Younger contributors to RRSPs show little grasp of investment knowledge. They purchase highly volatile emerging market mutual funds or no return Canada Savings Bonds but do not understand asset allocation or diversification. The portfolio needs growth, but it also needs security and lower risk to preserve capital. Blue chip equities, mortgage backed securities, strip bonds, and major market mutual funds will be superior long-term holdings. An RRSP is for buy and hold investments, not for speculation, market timing, or stock picking approaches.

Older investors in RRSPs seem to deny the need for some growth they can't get from fixed income securities. As a result, they run out of money before they run out of retirement.

They ignore the need to buy bonds in foreign currencies and staggered maturities to maximize returns and dollar protection. Worst of all, they ignore equities, ensuring that their RRSP can never reach its objectives.

More than 70% of RRSP investors never diversify outside of Canada, more than 55% never purchase equities, and fewer than 25% of women over the age of twenty-five have an RRSP.

Women are in particular need of aggressive RRSP investing. They live longer, earn less, and save less, and are as a result far more likely to end up in poverty upon retirement.

If Old Age Security and Canada Pension add up to only $12,000 a year in income and will be subject to a means test, clawbacks, or raised age qualification, it seems reasonable not to count on them for much in the future.

The RRSP on the other hand is a window of opportunity that is still open to most Canadians for now. It is imperative to forego other uses for your cash and savings and utilize the RRSP first. As Canadians, we simply have no other choice.

A recent study by the Canadian Institute of Actuaries clearly shows that the average private sector worker is only saving 6.8% of income in company pensions and RRSPs but needs a saving rate of 12-16% per annum of income to ensure adequate retirement income. A separate study in the fall of 1994 by a national accounting firm and The Canadian Institute of Financial Executives indicates that Canadian companies have unfunded retirement benefit liabilities of $54 billion and that 60% of all companies with pensions, in order to reduce costs, were moving from a defined benefit plan where you would get 60% of your average best five years' salary as a pension to a money purchase plan where the payout is not defined.

The actuary report shows that the 60% payout will be inadequate to meet people's needs over the next twenty to thirty years. Rather, a pension of 70-80% of earnings is needed now. More disturbing is the Financial Executive's study conclusion that 37% of the companies believe they can terminate retirement benefits at any time and without notice.

This clearly supports the argument that I have long presented that personal responsibility and not government or corporate pension sources is the way to go in the 1990s. You must learn to act for yourself and take responsibility by determining how much you will need and how to best achieve your retirement income goals.

Contrary to the government's view, RRSPs are not for the rich. They have other savings and investments that far exceed the value of RRSP benefits. While those with incomes over $150,000 annually make RRSP contributions (77% will contribute $13,200 or more this year), 83% of RRSP contributors earn less than $60,000 a year. It clearly is for the middle class, self-employed, and those who are not covered by pension plans. This is also the fastest growing sector of the workforce.

Clearly the failure to maximize RRSP contributions throughout the year is a debilitating long-term strategy. At early ages, the RRSP portfolio must be invested for growth and income and only adjusted for more income after age fifty-five. It must be a dynamic and aggressive vehicle that should remain sacrosanct and untouchable.

A level of personal discipline is essential. You will need a plan. So will your spouse. Retirement income splitting is essential to avoid the clawbacks on the age exemption and Old Age Security and to ensure personal independence. Separate incomes usually will be taxed at a lower rate. If each spouse is the designated beneficiary of the other's plan it will ensure a tax-free transfer on demise.

The period between 1995 and 2030 will see the number of those aged sixty-plus in Canada rise by 155% to become the overwhelming majority of the population. Because of poor planning, most of us will have to work at least until seventy years of age. At least 30% will end up in poverty. Most of those over sixty-five living in poverty (80%) will be women.

We still have the opportunity to act to prevent this. The problem will be to get Canadians to recognize the error of their ways and to avoid these classic RRSP errors.

SNOWBIRDS BEWARE

If you are a would-be snowbird, there are some basics you should understand about U.S. tax law and Canadian RRSPs.

- There's no U.S. equivalent to an RRSP. To the Internal Revenue Service, an RRSP is just another form of a bank account.

- The Canada-U.S. tax treaty, however, does allow Canadians residing in the U.S. to defer taxes on income accumulating within an RRSP.

- To win this deferral, expatriate Canadians must fill out an annual election, giving details of the plan, capital, and income growth while in the U.S. They must also file an annual return on foreign trusts, a form detailing any significant changes in the RRSP (this includes contributions, withdrawals, and income earned), and a new form under the U.S. Small Business Job Protection Act of 1996.

- Withdrawals from an RRSP by nonresidents face only a 25% withholding tax, a significant savings from the 50% rate charged Canadian residents. That withholding tax can also be applied as a credit against any U.S. taxes due on income.

- Withdrawals of up to $6,500 can, in fact, be tax free for anyone with no other income should you elect to file in Canada and make maximum use of personal exemptions.

Retirement Planning

"This is a rich land with a lazy people."
- Mordecai Richler, *Saturday Night Magazine*,
October 1995

No wonder Canadians don't make any money. They bought gold in 1979 at $961 an ounce because it was going to $310. They invested in 19 1/2% savings bonds in 1981 because after tax and inflation savings bonds produced a return of -2 3/4%, but it was a "guaranteed" negative cash flow. They bought real estate at the peak because it couldn't go down, based on a "Greater Fool Theory" that there was someone else out there dumber than you to sell it to.

WHY RETIREMENT MUST BE POSTPONED

"Blessed be he who expects nothing for he shall not be disappointed."
- Jonathan Swift

If you are a Canadian adult male aged sixty-five, statistically you have at least thirteen more years to live. For a woman, you have at least nineteen more years to live. More than one-sixth of you will surpass ninety years of age. Therefore, according to the way your holdings currently stand, you will probably run out of money before you run out of retirement.

In light of all the changes at the federal tax and corporate compensation level, you will not have enough capital invested correctly at age sixty-five to even think of retiring.

For Baby Boomers on down, the retirement lifestyle you were promised is virtually unattainable. It must look like a giant rip-off.

The Canada Pension Plan has an unfunded liability of $580 billion, more than double the national debt. The most someone aged fifty could expect on retirement is a dollar back for each one put in. Current CPP beneficiaries receive money out at a 6/1 ratio for each dollar contributed.

Old Age Security is subject to a clawback at $53,000. The loss of age exemption starting at $26,000 and the increased focus on pension and benefit reform ensures the longer term focus of taxation will be on those over sixty.

Companies are moving to increase early retirements, ensuring underfunding of pensions and lower payouts. Companies in Canada (60%) are moving to a money purchase pension plan from a defined benefit plan offering 60% of your best five years salary. This means you will have no idea how much you will get. Canadian companies currently have a $54 billion unfunded retirement benefit liability and 37% believe they can terminate these benefits at any time and without notice.

Having 60% will not be adequate anyway. The Canadian Institute of Actuaries reports that in 1997 retirees will need between 70-80% of their work income rising to 100% by 2005 — because of clawbacks, eliminations, and underfunding.

The average pensionable Canadian private sector worker saves only 6.8% in pensions and RRSPs with only 17% having $31,000 or more mostly invested in low growth GICs and nonperforming assets.

Today's retirees got their money from real estate and investments blessed by inflation. Current retirees saw their incomes rise 880% from 1960 to 1995 while Baby Boomers' income has only risen 34% and taxes have risen 1,167% since 1961.

Retirees had children early and gained massively from the real estate windfall in a long-term seller's market fueled by huge Baby Boomer demand.

Today, those who are forty to fifty-five years of age have less than their parents, and their children have even less. Government aid will not and cannot be there as the social safety net created in 1968 collapses from profligate spending and bloated government bureaucracy.

Low inflation, low growth, poor returns from fixed income investments, potential threats to RRSPs, increased taxes, a sharp decline in personal savings, parents having children later, a lack of long-term job security, and the failure to plan ahead all add up to a need to work and invest longer and more aggressively.

No Canadian over forty can possibly expect the same level of asset growth that their parents enjoyed. It must be a cause of substantial retirement and investment planning. Retirement, as we have come to expect it, is apparently no longer just obsolete but has become largely unaffordable for most Canadians.

The following chart highlights the national tragedy that has befallen us. Eighty-two percent of women

Canadian retirement situation in 1997

	Men 65+	Women 65+
Wealthy	1%	1%
Financially Secure	8%	2%
Must Continue Working	14%	11%
No Longer Alive	24%	4%
Required Financial Assistance	53%	82%

and 53% of men over sixty-five live on some form of public assistance .

The movement in the last budget away from clawbacks to withholding taxes on Old Age Security, reduced contribution limits for RRSPs, the reduction of the over-contribution limit, and the clear fact that with an unfunded liability of $580 billion the CPP will not be there for most of those under fifty has put the critical need for a personal retirement income plan into a new perspective.

Canadians must refocus their attention on retirement planning to avoid poverty.

Even those over sixty must learn that there must be dynamic growth in their retirement income portfolio until at least seventy-five years of age. This means at least 40% or more of their assets invested in equities. Failure to do so will result in seniors running out of money before they run out of retirement.

With the high probability of most Canadians living beyond seventy-five and reaching age ninety, there must be clear growth for another decade of investing.

If we look to company pension plans, we now find that 60% of Canadian retirement pensions are being converted from "defined benefit" pension plans paying 60% of the individual's best five years of earnings to "money purchase" pension plans where you have no idea what you will receive in income on retirement.

Retirees outside of Canada living in the United States will face 25% withholding tax on CPP and OAS. Those retiring outside of North America must file a world income statement return with Revenue Canada by July 1, of each year, or face losing all pension income from Canada.

Women must learn to save at least 15% of earnings until age fifty, and 20% from fifty to sixty-five years of age. They must invest to earn returns 6% greater than men and this cannot be achieved via GICs, savings bonds, or savings accounts.

Every Canadian is in need of a personal retirement income plan for themselves and their spouse. There can no longer be an exception to this.

Nineteen ninety-seven may be the year of the tax accountant, but it is also the year of the financial planner or advisor. Act now to avoid poverty in your retirement years.

WHAT IS RETIREMENT PLANNING?

"Too many Canadians believe retirement planning is lining up on February 28 in front of a bank teller to buy a GIC."

The essence of successful retirement planning is ensuring that you will have enough income to maintain you and your spouse or family in the lifestyle you had during your working years when you retire, in a place where you want to retire, for as long as you are retired. This may involve managing income from personal savings, income from the conversion of your Registered Retirement Savings Plan (RRSP) into a Registered Retirement Income Fund (RRIF), income from an active investment portfolio, income from a company pension plan or a government pension plan or social security programs (such as Canada Pension Plan or Old Age Security payments), and perhaps, active income from a second career or entrepreneurial business you may have started.

Retirement Plan Facts

The average RRSP holdings are $31,000. Someone thirty-five years of age who wishes to retire at the age of sixty-five with an annual income of $25,000 from retirement savings to add to the $12,000 per year from CPP and OAP will need to have $525,000 in an RRSP. That's $5,060 per year for thirty years compounding at 7%. That's $195 every two weeks that must be put away.

RETIREMENT - FACT AND FICTION ABOUT THE SOCIAL SAFETY NET IN CANADA

With all the discussion about the decrepit state of the Canada Pension Plan, it may be useful to step back for a minute and destroy some misconceptions about social security programs in Canada, and explore what our government should be doing to protect the most financially disadvantaged groups in Canada.

Myth #1: Social security programs such as the Canada Pension Plan (CPP) and Old Age Security (OAS) insure pensioners against poverty and financial risk.

Reality: Benefit formulas in all of these programs are arbitrary, redefined frequently (often in each successive Federal Budget), and subject to strategic manipulation and budget constraints. What is more, Canadians are now paying more to receive less benefit. Already, CPP premiums have increased to 5.8% of income from 4.0% over the last several years. In order to rescue the solvency of the plan, experts agree that these premiums must approach 11% of income. Canadians are only now beginning to realize that by themselves, CPP and OAS benefits are no guarantee or protection from anything except poverty.

Myth #2: Only the federal government is capable of protecting pensioners against financial risks in their old age.

Reality: Past performance has proven that most governments are incapable of managing their own finances, let alone yours. Leaving it up to the government to look after you financially is a dangerous mistake. At present, CPP has a $580 billion unfunded liability representing the cost of future pension liabilities not currently funded. Rather than continually restricting the ability of individual Canadians to plan, save, and invest to finance their own retirement, efforts should be made to help this to happen. Except in the most extreme cases, it would relieve the government of a huge responsibility it cannot handle and would also end the sense of retirement complacency it wrongly fosters in Canadian citizens.

Myth #3: Individuals are myopic, but governments take the long view.

Reality: Governments in all developed countries (Canada is no exception) repeatedly make decisions about social security programs based on short-run exigencies rather than long-run benefits to their society. One example is the use of early retirement programs as a temporary solution to unemployment that in the long-run costs the economy big time in lost labour and the public treasury in large pension payouts.

Myth #4: Older Canadians are the most poor so social security programs to alleviate poverty should be focussed on the elderly.

Reality: In many parts of Canada, poverty rates are higher among younger people than the elderly. Young families with small children are among the poorest of all. Therefore, targeting young families with children is a better measure for alleviating poverty than focussing on pension reform for the elderly.

Myth #5: CPP and OAS are an effective way of redistributing income in a fair way to elderly Canadians who are poor.

Reality: Even if benefit formulas for these, or other

programs, look progressive, four factors often neutralize most of the progressive effect. The first people to be covered when new plans are started are often middle and upper income groups, and they usually receive large transfers. Second, the longer life expectancy of wealthy people distorts the progressivity of programs when redistribution is calculated on a lifetime rather than an annual basis. Third, ceilings on taxable earnings keep the lid on tax differences between rich and poor. Finally, when benefit formulae are earnings related or subject to manipulation, upper income groups often benefit disproportionately.

Myth #6: All Canadians will receive equal benefits.

Reality: Most public pay-as-you-go pension plans (Canada's CPP included) provide the largest net benefits to workers who are thirty to fifty years old when the schemes are introduced. Successive generations of Canadians are unlikely to receive the same level of benefits by the time they are ready to retire many years in the future. According to an OECD study in Canada in 1980, there were 7.1 working Canadians for each retiree; by 2000, there will be 5.3 working Canadians for each retiree. In effect, as the system matures and the demographic transition of Canada's population proceeds, future generations are financing current pensioners from a declining tax base.

RESEARCH - CPP - WHAT'S GONE WRONG?

Why is the Canada Pension Plan in trouble? Although, it is primarily the consequence of fiscal mismanagement by the federal government in Canada, it is also a result of steadily rising life expectancy, a trend toward a lower retirement age, and declining fertility rates combined with a lack of political will to recognize these trends and make the necessary changes. However, this is not a problem found only in Canada; it is a worldwide phenomenon.

Consider that:

• on average, men now live for fifteen years after their normal mandatory retirement age of sixty-five while women live almost twenty years more; and,

• in 1990, 15.6% of Canada's population was over sixty years of age, but by the year 2150, this number is expected to double to 31%.

Most frustrating is that this is not a problem that has suddenly appeared without notice. Population growth and demographic trends are hardly sudden developments. Canadian society is characteristic of a group of world economies which are essentially middle aged with rapidly aging populations, have substantial public pension programs providing widespread coverage with costs that will soar, and will have increasing dependency rates over the next thirty years.

Yet, with all the talk of the CPP being insolvent, what

are the solutions? Before we start casting blame for the current CPP mess, perhaps we should step back and review what the objective of an old age security system should be. It should have three functions: insurance, saving, and income redistribution.

The World Bank, in a 1994 Policy Research Report entitled, "Averting the Old Age Crisis," recommends separating the redistribution, insurance, and saving functions into separate and distinct programs because of the proven inability of most countries (both developing and developed) to sustain a single plan incorporating all three elements.

The World Bank report highlights the importance of what it calls a "3 pillar system" of old age security. These pillars are:

1. a publicly managed system with mandatory participation with the limited goal of reducing poverty among the old and those least capable to supporting themselves (the "redistribution" function);

2. a privately managed mandatory savings program designed to preserve a satisfactory quality of retirement life (the "insurance" function); and,

3. a voluntary savings plan for those wishing to supplement retirement income (the "savings" function).

Based on this report, what should the Canadian government do to reform pension policy? Three things:

1. reform the public plan (CPP) by raising the retirement age, eliminating rewards for early retirement and penalties for late retirement, reducing benefit levels and making the benefit structure flatter to emphasize the poverty reduction function, lowering the tax rate and broadening the tax base

2. create a mandatory privately managed system with increased contribution limits

3. promote any form of voluntary savings (primarily in the form of RRSPs)

The recent Federal Budget completely ignores the need for immediate changes to CPP and defers any discussion or recommendations regarding CPP until a study is released in 1997 on this problem. Moreover, there is no mention of any moves to create a mandatory privately managed system.

Finally, it only deals with RRSPs and moves completely in the wrong direction. Although carry-forwards have been extended indefinitely for unused contributions from 1991 on, RRSP limits have been capped at $13,500 until 2004, and then they rise only to $15,500 in 2005. Self-directed fees for RRSPs are no longer tax deductible, and for everyone currently age sixty-eight or younger, the maximum age for RRSP contributions has been reduced to age sixty-nine from age seventy-one.

Because of the importance of this issue, we will produce a follow up analysis of the CPP reform plan when it is presented in order to assess how well it conforms to the World Bank recommendations and the needs of Canadians.

ULTIMATE WEALTH - A STRATEGIC RETIREMENT

As more Canadians begin to realize they cannot possibly rely on government pensions or corporate benefits for a secure retirement, they have adopted a strategic approach to a transitional retirement.

It is transitional because they either work or earn expanded retirement income to a minimum age of sixty-nine and a maximum age of seventy-five. It is strategic as it is a series of action plans to insure capital preservation, maximum investment returns, and the lowest possible tax liability.

Our multistep approach to Ultimate Wealth should include most of the following:

1. While the house is a major asset, it must be used for investment and tax benefits. We should leverage against the property to at least 20% of its value to purchase high grade investments such as blue chip, major market, equity mutual funds, double A or better grade government bonds and mortgage backed securities, and low risk, high return tax ameliorated investments such as mutual fund limited partnerships and developmental oil and gas limited partnerships. The house can also be used for leveraging a systematic withdrawal plan.

2. In your financial planning, insure that you have prop-

er asset allocation with a minimum of 25% equities until age seventy-five. With a proper growth structure between age sixty-five and seventy-five, diversification will reduce risk and enhance returns.

3. Learn not to see CPP and OAS as entitlements. With clawbacks and withholding taxes in 1997, many people will be getting a smaller cheque. Rely on your investments to maintain your lifestyle.

4. As you age, most costs such as travel, food, and clothing for work decline; only health costs rise. Learn to scale back overheads, conserve cash and reinvest this money for financial security. Use all tax refunds for reinvestment not consumption.

5. If you reach sixty-five, you have a very high probability of reaching seventy-eight. If you are seventy, plan your income to at least eighty-five, and at seventy-five plan for ninety. This means you need growth in your portfolio at least ten years longer than you figured.

6. of women and 60% of men over age sixty and under sixty-five claim CPP. This is a foolhardy approach. Plan to work at least part-time to the age of sixty-nine to maximize earned income for your RRSP, to give you a good mental challenge, and to build your capital and CPP base.

7. Entrepreneurship is especially good after age sixty. It allows you to generate post-retirement income that quali-

fies for your RRSP until age sixty-nine. If you have a home business, it also acts to create tax deductions out of previously nondeductible expenses such as property taxes, house insurance, and hydro. Entrepreneurship keeps your brain alive, and either or both spouses can be involved.

8. A spousal business for the lower or no-income spouse is ideal for income splitting. By giving both spouses separate earned income, each ends up with a retirement income stream and lower taxes can result. It enhances the couple's financial security long term.

9. Measure your income now to determine your long-term projected shortfall. Add up the income stream after tax from company pensions, CPP, OAS, and investments. Then figure out how much you need to maintain the lifestyle you want, especially if you are in good health and have many years ahead.

10. Become computer literate and learn to use financial planning software. You're never too old to learn, and it's very simple. It will help you immensely.

11. If under age sixty-nine, borrow to maximize RRSP contributions, including spousal plan contributions.

12. The new rules of saving for the 1990s are: If you are under the age of fifty, save 15% of your income; if you are over the age of fifty, save 20%.

RETIRING PROPERLY TRANSITION & NOT QUITTING

The process of retiring in the 1990s is not one of suddenly retiring from a job at age sixty-five and drawing retirement income. Canada's changing demographics and economics now mean that we are living longer and we will work longer (probably until age seventy) and then gradually phase out of the workplace.

Most Canadians will go through a transition from full-time employment to part-time or contract employment to self-employment and then home business.

With the transformation from OAS clawbacks to withholding taxes at source, the inadequacies of most company pensions paying only 60% of your best five years salary (when you will need 75% minimum), and the gross underfunding of CPP, every adult Canadian needs a new twelve-step strategy that is in line with the retirement transition process of the 1990s. This strategy will remain valid at least until 2015.

1. Save at least 15% of net income to age fifty. This should rise to 20% from fifty to sixty-five years of age. This is especially important for women.

2. Cut costs of living after age fifty. Focus on cash management. As you gradually withdraw from work, you will need less money for travel, clothes, entertainment, food, etc. Save the cost differences and reinvest the cash.

3. Learn to forget about CPP. Don't even count on your

company pension as an income stream. Consider them only as a bonus. This will force you to be more aggressive in your retirement income planning.

4. Use your house as a source for leverage. Once you are an "empty nester," sell the house and downsize your accommodation. Use the principal for a systematic withdrawal plan to augment cash flow and reduce taxes.

5. Follow a plan of asset allocation and diversification. This will reduce risk and preserve capital significantly. Asset allocation is the single most important influence on your financial returns. It determines up to 91% of your portfolio growth.

6. Plan your second career. You can work at least part-time until age seventy-one to insure there is additional earned income for your RRSP.

7. Establish a home business. Do this as early as possible and get your spouse involved. It is ideal for income splitting, reducing taxes by making a portion of household costs deductible, and for increasing income on retirement.

8. Create a spousal business. No matter how modest, it provides an income splitting opportunity. If there is a spouse not working outside the home, it represents a great vehicle for tax reduction, RRSP planning, and retirement fun. Insure each spouse has a separate RRSP.

9. Invest for growth at least until age seventy-five. Do

not reduce the equity components of the portfolio until seventy-five or you will run out of money before you run out of retirement.

10. Measure and quantify all your retirement income sources - this includes government, company, and personal investment income - and determine the shortfall before it is too late.

11. Borrow for your RRSP. This will allow you to maximize the contribution each year. Remember, $525,000 in RRSPs provides only $25,000 in income a year for twenty years of retirement. Most of us need $1 million in an RRSP to retire in comfort.

12. Learn to be computer literate. Use financial planning software to take charge of your retirement.

Projected Level of the Seniors Benefit in 2001		
Income from other sources[1]	Tax-free Benefit	
	Single Seniors	Elderly couples
	(dollars per year)	
0	11,420	18,440
5,000	8,920	15,940
10,000	6,420	13,440
15,000	5,160	10,940
20,000	5,160	10,320
25,000	5,160	10,320
30,000	4,350	9,510

35,000	3,350	8,510
40,000	2,350	7,510
45,000	1,350	6,510
50,000	350	5,510
60,000	-	3,510
70,000	-	1,510
80,000	-	-

[1] Includes income from CPP/QPP, but excludes income from OAS/GIS which the Seniors benefit replaces.

Asset Allocation to Retirement

Asset Class	Years to Retirement				
	30	20	15	10	5
Cash	0%	0%	0%	0%	0%
Fixed Income	10%	15%	20%	25%	35%
Equities	70%	65%	60%	55%	50%
Hard Assets	20%	20%	20%	20%	15%

Asset Class	Retirement Period		
	Early	Middle	Late
Cash	10%	10%	10%
Fixed Income	40%	55%	60%
Equities	40%	35%	25%
Hard Assets	10%	5%	5%

WOMEN NEED TO PLAN AHEAD FOR COMFORTABLE RETIREMENT

Only 10% of today's working women will be covered by a private pension plan other than CPP. Yet today's women earn an average of only 72.5% of what men do and live six to eight years longer.

More than 80% of those living in poverty who are older than sixty-five years of age are women. Women also make up 65% of those living in poverty and who are younger than forty.

Women must learn to be more financially knowledgeable and aggressive in their investment activity.

A recent U.S. study by Susan Forward entitled "Money Demons: Keep Them From Sabotaging Your Relationships and Your Life" points to the fact that women find themselves often overwhelmed by personal conflicts over money with male partners.

It is not unusual for women to regularly pay off their partner's bad debts or turn their earnings over to a spouse despite a history of mismanagement and profligate spending.

In most families, real estate is still held in the name of the male as a matter of trust; joint ownership is a more recent phenomenon.

True independence and liberation for women comes only from personal financial independence, not from feeling or being financially used.

Yet how are women to find this financial independence?

A *Money Magazine* U.S. study and a *Globe and Mail* report about mutual funds both concluded that women do not get as good service or as much respect from large financial institutions and brokers as men do. Brokers and bankers spend more time with men, ask them more questions, treat them more seriously, and try harder to land them as customers.

While both studies concluded that banking and brokerage services were less than wonderful for women, women still tended to be more dependent on the institutions and less willing to get independent financial advice.

Teachers, nurses, and white collar supervisors, occupations commonly dominated by women, tend to rely more on their pensions, bonds, GICs, and local banks than most. Yet their financial investment performance proved to be worse than most despite incomes in the $50,000 to $60,000 a year range. They should be saving 12.5 to 15% of their incomes by age forty-five, yet most save 2 to 5%.

An age-based plan should be as follows:

Ages 24 to 39: Set up your RRSP. Make systematic withdrawals each month for mutual funds and investments. Invest each month. Maximize dividend and capital gain income. Plan to acquire your own home by the time you are thirty. Have at least 65% of your assets in equities, equity mutual funds, and real estate.

Ages 39 to 55: Maximize RRSP and pension contributions. Your savings rate should be at least 1% per month. Take lower-risk equities down to 50% of assets; cash and treasury bills for children's education at 10-15%. Salary earnings and business income should exceed investment earnings.

Ages 55 to 69: Investment earnings must exceed salary and business income. Equities decline to 40% of holdings. Capital preservation and conservative income growth is key. Plan to have retirement income of 75% of your current cost of living as a basic threshold. Downsize real estate holdings. Ensure a will and estate planning is in place. Maximize RRSP until seventy-one.

Following this plan should help you attain real peace of mind and long-term security.

Estate Planning

WHAT IS ESTATE PLANNING?

Most people don't like to think about estate planning because it reminds us all of our own mortality. However, it is important if you care about your spouse, children, parents, other family members, or special friends to think about your estate and how you want to protect it.

Effective estate planning is the process, which should involve both spouses and children, of understanding and managing the important legal, financial, and tax issues related to protecting the value of your estate following your death and preparing for the orderly handling, administration, and disposition of your estate to heirs or designates according to the dictates of your will or, if you do not have a will, a court's ruling.

A proper estate plan must, therefore, address five key issues:

1. Beneficiaries: Ensuring a consistent standard of living and providing for the financial needs of your surviving spouse and dependents or heirs.

2. Control: Ensuring that your estate plan is structured to maintain control over the assets to the greatest extent possible.

3.   Distribution: Planning and directing that each of the assets covered by the estate plan is ultimately directed to the people or institutions to which you intended they go.

4.   Taxes: Minimizing the amount of tax that must be paid by the estate at the time of transfer.

5.   Business Interests: If the estate includes an operating family business or other type of venture which is intended to continue, the estate plan should outline the principals upon which it can survive.

For the record, here is a concise definition:

Estate: All the assets a person possesses at the time of death, such as securities, real estate, business interests, physical possessions and cash.

Finally, perhaps the most common reason for estate planning is to avoid (as much as possible) family feuds after you are gone over how your estate is to be managed or distributed.

HOW TO DO IT!

Like tax planning, estate planning is a very complex process. It requires the assistance of a trusted professional financial advisor and, in some cases, detailed legal and accounting advice. However, there is a growing awareness of the need to plan for estate purposes, and many new options are opening up for consideration by more and more Canadians who are being proactive by preparing estate plans.

For our purposes, it is most appropriate to identify some of the most common estate planning products which are available and explain briefly how they work.

A proper estate plan must therefore address five key issues:

1. Beneficiaries: life insurance, gifts to family members

2. Control: rollover, charitable gifts

3. Distribution: wills (to be discussed separately in wills section)

4. Taxes: trusts, estate freeze, offshore investing

5. Business Interests: corporation

PLAN TO REDUCE PROBATE FEES

People seem to be more concerned about possible estate or capital taxes and probate fees than ever before.

We have no estate taxes in Canada yet. However, there are deemed disposition on death taxes (capital gains taxes on the estate).

The process begins with spouses holding assets such as homes or cottages jointly. The asset passes to the survivor tax-free and without probate. A testamentary trust can be established so that on the death of the second partner it can flow to the children.

Insurance is of particular benefit when there are reasonable assets in the estate. Costs are not low, but the benefits of an exempt policy are that it pays the deemed disposition taxes and leaves a residual that is also nontaxable in the estate.

Independent advice from an insurance agent and financial planner are advisable here. You can give cash tax-free to children and grandchildren and other assets at fair market value.

An estate freeze freezes the value of your assets at today's values and freezes any growth in their value. This is particularly useful in a family business to ensure an orderly succession plan.

Any capital gains that occur between the time the business started to the time of the freeze are also frozen, so no capital gains tax is paid until the husband and wife are dead. This assumes they have set up a so-called second-to-die provision in their estate plan. The freeze ensures future growth in the company takes place in the hands of the children only.

With cottages, as noted, joint ownership is best. Until April 1995, you could file for your $100,000 exemption, and if each spouse is a joint owner and has the exemption, $200,000 in gains may be exempt from January 1, 1992. If you haven't used it you still have until April 30, 1997, to file.

The family trust usually results in one child buying out the others to get the cottage or leaving it all to the children and grandchildren to split the tax.

Asset protection offshore trusts are advisable for those in business with credit risks and assets of more than $1 million.

These trusts can protect you from creditors' liability lawsuits and marital breakdown.

You transfer assets to a trust outside your control. Your family can benefit from the wealth and you can be involved in its management, but it is shielded from creditors because it is no longer yours.

The trust should be irrevocable, but you could give the trustee discretion to collapse the trust, perhaps after ten years if it is no longer needed. Holdings can go to the beneficiary, including you.

Set-up costs can run from $5,000 to $20,000 with 1% per annum for administration.

RRSPs and RRIFs can't be held in offshore trusts. Putting Canadian real estate into an asset protection trust defeats the trust's purpose because it's easy for the creditors to trace and track the property through Canadian courts.

There are at least twenty offshore options, but the eight best are Cayman Islands, Cook Islands, Bahamas, Belize, Gibraltar, Mauritius, Turks, and Caicos Islands. I like Cayman and Cook Islands the best.

Be sure to have a protector in your trust to veto trustee decisions and replace the trustee if need be. The best option for protector is a spouse or adult child.

ESTATE PLANNING TIPS

Every adult Canadian over the age of thirty-five with

assets should consider preparing a proper estate plan to ensure the orderly transfer of assets to intended beneficiaries upon death. While none of us relishes thinking about our mortality, we have no choice.

Governments at all levels are looking to the transfer of over one trillion dollars between generations over the next decade as a potential major windfall. While most provincial jurisdictions already have probate fees ranging from a flat fee to 1.5% of the value of the estate over $50,000, this will be a major area of tax increases.

Federally, we also have a capital gains tax on the estate called a "deemed disposition on death" creating a substantial tax liability that could result in the family being forced to sell assets to pay the tax if proper precautions have not been taken.

Fortunately you have many good strategies to consider and help from advisors who can make a difference.

A lawyer, accountant, insurance agent, and financial advisor are all part of the estate planning team. Each performs a critical role. The lawyer will draft the will, power of attorney, and trust agreements to protect the assets. The accountant foresees the tax liabilities and recommends strategy to mitigate them. The insurance agent provides the much needed "last to die" policy or "exempt life" to cover taxes and provide a larger "free estate." The financial advisor provides the investment and resources to ensure a proper estate is available at the lowest tax cost.

To minimize tax liabilities on death, a number of options should be considered:

1. Ensure that all property, especially real estate, is in the name of both spouses to avoid probate, deemed disposition taxes, and to be certain it passes directly to the spouse.

2. Consider liquidating unneeded assets before death and converting them to cash which can be given tax free to family members.

3. Establish proper "exempt" life insurance that is a tax-free income shelter and provides funds to pay any taxes owed at a discounted cost as you have paid for it in advance over the past twenty years.

4. Consider establishing a testamentary trust in your will to direct the assets to children while continuing to allow income to be earned on them for years.

5. Ensure your RRSP, RRIF, life insurance policies, and annuities have a named spousal beneficiary, excluding them from the estate and permitting a tax-free rollover without probate.

6. Each individual can earn over $6,450 of income tax free because of your base tax credit. If you create a trust and make a "preferred beneficiary election," each grandchild that is such a beneficiary can receive up to $6,450 of income with no tax liability, but the income must be paid out.

7.   Qualifying small business corporations and farms can use the $500,000 capital gains exemption to shelter gains, and family farms can be rolled over to the children tax free.

8.   If there has been a divorce, a new will must be drawn and the prior one revoked.

9.   Determine how much will be needed for funeral costs and how much cash the survivor will need in the first months after your demise. Ensure that substantial cash is immediately available to the surviving spouse to pay all liabilities.

10. Act now and update the plan approximately every three years or when major tax changes occur. We must be proactive even when anticipating our own death.

Remember:
1.   a will — updated every three years
2.   a power of attorney for financial affairs in the event of incapacitation
3.   a personal care proxy and living will for personal care if you are unable to make medical decisions for yourself

These three documents are your "legals for life."

ESTATE PLANNING - THE ULTIMATE GIFT

When you spend as much time as I do traversing this vast country from one coast to the other, it makes it a little easier for me than for most financial professionals to get a sense of "the big picture." In a country where all too often we are defined by the differences that divide us, there is occasionally an amazing degree of consensus. And one of the big things going on these days is the rapid emergence of estate planning as a key financial planning issue for many Canadians.

Historically, estate planning has been the least understood aspect of a comprehensive financial plan - often completely overlooked. I think that there are two reasons.

1. The first is the myth that estate planning is a complex and expensive process.

2. The second myth is that it is an exercise which is only relevant for wealthy families.

Estate Planning Is a Hot Topic

Looking ahead to 1997, it seems entirely likely that I will conduct as many estate planning seminars as I do for tax or retirement planning, investment strategy, or family finances. So what is going on? Why is there such a fuss all of a sudden?

Generally speaking, I think it can be summarized as follows:

- First, the amazing strength of the bull market we have experienced during the 1990s has meant that many astute Canadian investors have made big money over the last four or five years. So now, as they move toward retirement, they are wondering how to protect this newly acquired wealth.

- Second, the "Baby Boom" generation (the first of whom turned fifty years of age in 1996) now have families whose welfare is weighing heavily on their minds.

- Finally, as families see their financial assets grow, they become aware for the first time of the potentially crippling impact of taxation on their estate.

In fact, one common refrain that I am hearing a lot of these days is that it is entirely possible for many Canadians that, on their death, their estate will pay more in tax than they would have paid in income tax over their entire life. How about that for a reality check?

Beneficiaries: Ensuring a consistent standard of living and providing for the financial needs of your surviving spouse, dependents, or heirs.

Control: Ensuring that your estate plan is structured to maintain control over the assets to the greatest extent possible.

Distribution: Planning and directing that each of the

assets covered by the plan is ultimately directed to the people or institutions to which you intended they go.

Taxes: Minimizing the amount of tax that must be paid by the estate at the time of transfer. This can take the form of income tax (on moneys received by your beneficiaries), capital gains tax (remember the "deemed disposition on death" principle), probate fees (the cost of settling your estate), or legal and administration fees (associated with managing your estate after your demise). Also, don't forget about hefty funeral expenses.

Business Interests: Outlining the principles and establishing a plan which will allow for the survival and prosperity of an operating family business.

So what tools do you have in your estate planning arsenal?

Your advisors should include a lawyer, accountant, insurance agent, and financial advisor.

- The required documentation you need includes a properly drawn, up-to-date "will" and a "power of attorney" for both property assets and personal care.

- Depending on circumstances and your personal net worth, your estate may also benefit from a "living trust," a corporation (to effect an estate freeze), or life insurance (to be used for income replacement purposes, to fund business buyouts, or to pay income tax arising on death).

One last thing to bear in mind: Estate planning is critical to intergenerational financial planning. But all too often an important aspect is missed. If you ask a professional advisor to define estate planning, in one sentence, generally they would say something like "the process of protecting and preserving the value and financial assets within a client's estate." Talk like this drives me crazy. It completely misses the point of the exercise.

The only reason that more and more Canadians are so concerned about estate planning is that they have learned during the 1990s that in order to get ahead financially, they are having to work themselves to death. More responsibility, declining real income, longer working hours - this all adds up to major-league stress. For most Canadians, the only reason for putting up with this routine is the hope of trying to provide a better standard of living for their families.

Therefore, to my way of thinking, the objective is not simply to protect and preserve the value and financial assets within a client's estate. What is the point of having a huge bank account if it just sits there without benefiting anyone? The real objective is to develop a plan for transferring the value of your estate to surviving family members in a way that will actually enhance the quality of their lives and allow them to use the money wisely.

PROBATE FEES VARY WIDELY BETWEEN PROVINCES

Probate of a will is not required by law but by third-party institutions such as banks and trust companies to make sure your executors have the right to act.

Financial institution deposits, real estate, and shares in a public company require probate.

However, you can transfer title on real estate with a copy of a death certificate and a notarized copy of the will.

If you designate the beneficiaries of insurance policies, RRSPs, RRIFs, annuities, and pensions, proceeds will be paid outside the estate with no probate required.

Other options to consider: If you have a large estate, set up an Alberta corporation. It's the cheapest common law province to probate a will. The holding company will be a private corporation.

A second option is to have several wills, one for property such as bank accounts, stocks, and real estate that need probate, the other for everything else. Make sure the wills do not conflict and accidentally revoke the other.

A third choice is an inter vivos trust set up while you are alive to hold assets. It is a separate legal entity not subject to probate fees. A home would not lose its tax-exempt status as principal residence if held in a trust. It is superior from a tax-planning perspective.

Ontario has increased probate fees on wills by 300%. They are now 0.5% of the first $50,000, 1.5% of everything thereafter, and $15,000 per million. It could take anywhere from six to fifteen months to probate a will. The probate system is designed for the court to establish that the will is valid.

For many residents, the principal asset may be the family home, which can pass without probate from spouse to spouse simply by a right to survivorship detailed in a will. There are no taxes to pay.

Here are the probate fees for other provinces:

Newfoundland: $50 for the first $1,000, then $4 per $1,000 thereafter.

Nova Scotia: $75 for the first $10,000, $500 on estates over $200,000, then $3 per $1,000 thereafter.

Prince Edward Island: $50 on the first $10,000, rising to $400 on estates of $100,000, then $4 per $1,000.

New Brunswick: $5 per $1,000.

Quebec: No fees; usually $45 for registration.

Manitoba: $5 per $1,000.

Saskatchewan: $12 on the first $9,000, then $6 per $1,000.

Alberta: $25 on the first $10,000 to $6,000 on estates more than $1 million.

A Test of Wills

Baby boomers' expectations about inheriting money from their parents.

How many expect to have a disagreement with relatives about inheritance?	21%
How many expect to receive an inheritance from their parents?	62%
How many believe that parents are obligated to leave an estate behind?	16%
How many believe they deserve an inheritance?	60%
How many have discussed inheritance with their parents?	54%

Source: First Interstate Bank Trust; Private Banking Group

LIFE INSURANCE IS LIKE A PARACHUTE

You have to have it before you need it! According to the Canadian Life and Health Insurance Association, Canadians currently own slightly more than $1.5 trillion in life insurance ($743 billion in individual life policies and $797 billion in group life policies). On a per capita basis, Canadian wage earners' average insurance coverage is $52,300.

In contrast, Americans carry a total of $16.4 trillion in insurance which, on a per capital basis, means that the average American carries slightly over $60,300. This compares with the Japanese, who are the world's most heavily insured workers, with $235,000 coverage per person.

The bottom line is that Canadians, for the most part, are underinsured with incomes and financial assets that are not well protected.

Death and Taxes

The saying goes, "There are two things certain in life, death and taxes." Yet some people say, "I don't believe in life insurance." If other people are dependent on you financially or otherwise (children, spouse, or business partners), then you need life insurance.

"There has been an accident. Names will not be released until next of kin are notified." You have heard it before. Death is not a philosophical argument. Death either happens suddenly as in a plane crash, highway accident, or fire, or it happens gradually, as in illnesses like cancer, AIDS, a hereditary disease, a "freak" disease, or old age. If you are in any doubt, read the obituaries in your newspaper.

There are only two questions: First, and most important, how much? Second, what kind?

How much life insurance should you buy? If insuring your home, how much insurance would you buy? The bank insists that it be for full replacement value of the house. If your house is destroyed, it can be replaced. If you lose your job or business, or become seriously ill, there may be a period of hardship. If you die, it's final. You won't recover. Your dependents will require the income you would have earned. Many falsely believe that employer group insurance covers that need. It is usually insufficient, as many widows and widowers have discovered too late. People who have been "downsized" or left their employment discover that group life coverage ends. (Most employer group plans include a thirty-day right, without proof of good health, to continue coverage with a whole life policy. This is an important right if any health issues would prevent obtaining coverage.)

Starting Point

To determine the amount of insurance for most young families the starting point should be the replacement of current annual income. Do the math: How much do you expect to earn over the next twenty years? If you died, how would your single spouse replace the income you would have earned? Some of the common responses I hear to that question are: "They can get remarried, live on RSP savings, get a job, sell the house and move into an apartment, move in with their with parents." What all these responses are really saying is that there won't be enough money. Thousands of families have experienced financial hardship because of job loss or business failure in the last five years. If you die, it's permanent.

What are your dependents' needs over the next ten years? The next twenty years? Forty years from now? Almost certainly, your need and reasons for life insurance will change over time.

A family earning $80,000 per year may need an insurance plan of at least $1 million. If it sounds like a fortune, it's not. You will likely earn more than a million over the next twelve years.

Should the insurance be Whole Life, Universal Life, Yearly Renewable Term (YRT), Term Five, Term Ten, Term to 100, or some other offering?

Whole Life is simple. Your premium will be fixed for your lifetime. The insurance company will make investments on your behalf and guarantee you a cash surrender value. If you view Whole Life as an investment, it typically gives poor returns. Whole Life is a permanent type of policy.

Universal Life is level term, permanent life insurance plus an investment account. It allows you to make investment decisions. Investment growth is tax-free and premiums can be paid with "before tax dollars. Cash assets can be passed on to the next generation tax-free. "UL" policies are flexible and provide many tax advantages. If you have maximized your RRSP, this type of plan may be just what you are looking for.

Term Life policies are simply increasing term insurance and typically are purchased in five- and ten-year terms. These plans will be less expensive than Whole or Universal at the beginning, then increase on scheduled terms. Insurance will become much more expensive past age sixty-five. Most term plans are convertible in whole or in part to permanent insurance; each company will specify this in the contract. Term insurance usually expires at age seventy-five and rates vary. Be sure that you know what the renewal rates are. Total premiums over twenty years can be more than $10,000 apart!

Term policies can also be purchased as twenty, twenty-five, and Term to 100 coverage. When searching for the right policy for you, here are some points to be aware of:

Life Insurance Comparison for $1 Million (monthly rates)

	Whole Life level premium	Universal min. premium	Universal max. premium	10 yr. term yrs. 1-10	10 yr. term yrs. 11-20	10 yr. term yrs. 21-30	10 yr. term yrs. 31-40*
Male 35	$706	$296	$1,694	$104	$207	$533	$1,485
Male 40	$984	$406	$2,045	$140	$328	$869	$2,245

Note that term insurance becomes very expensive at $2,245 per month!

Total Premiums over 30 years

	Whole Life level premium	Universal min. premium	Universal max. premium	10 yr. term yrs. 1-10			
Male 35	$254,160	$106,380	$610,080	$101,280			
Male 40	$354,240	$146,280	$736,080	$160,440			

	Whole Life level premium	Universal min. premium	Universal max. premium	10 yr. term yrs. 1-10	10 yr. term yrs. 11-20	10 yr. term yrs. 21-30	10 yr. term yrs. 31-40*
Female 35	$622	$246	$1,485	$90	$151	$362	$964
Female 40	$846	$312	$1,782	$109	$226	$587	$1,649

Note that term insurance becomes very expensive at $1,649 per month!

Total Premiums over 30 years

	Whole Life level premium	Universal min. premium	Universal max. premium	10 yr. term yrs. 1-10			
Female 35	$223,920	$88,560	$534,600	$72,360			
Female 40	$304,560	$112,320	$641,520	$110,640			

Always consider current and future premium rates. It is usually possible to combine permanent and term insurance in one policy. Depending on your needs and the time period, the least expensive life insurance may not be "the best." As many seniors will attest, the best type of life insurance is affordable and still in force when you die. Many term policies provide a right to convert part or all coverage to permanent insurance. Coverage can be reduced as years pass if your need for coverage changes - E&OE.

* most term insurance expires at age 75.

1. Look for guaranteed rates. If rates are not guaranteed, be sure you understand how the variables would affect premiums. For example, some policies sold in the '80s were based on interest rates being over 10%. Those policies now have problems because interest rates are well below 10%.

2. Many people have too little insurance. Someone said that Canadians are overinsured. It's not true. Would it be more terrible for your survivors to have more than they needed or too little? Remember that some of the things you do "for free" would have to be hired out.

3. Don't wait too long to decide. There is always a risk of dying. You save nothing by waiting and putting your family's future at risk.

4. Don't be dependent on a group plan. These include employer, bank (mortgage or credit card), alumni, or association plans. In the case of mortgage life insurance, if you change lenders, you must apply

for new coverage at your new age. Group plans are valuable extra insurance only. Group plans also may exclude some causes of death. Some group plans only cover accidental death. That means if you die of an illness or disease, you are not covered!

5. Life insurance must be part of any good financial plan. Love it or hate it. The biggest error many people make is being underinsured. You should review your needs every five years and at every significant financial and life change.

6. Be careful. A professional should help you decide what and how to buy life insurance. Ask which companies they represent and who they deal with most often.

7. Look after your health. You are not the only one who will decide about your life insurance. You must be in good health to receive the best rates. If your health is impaired, you should still apply, some-times to more than one company. However, being approved can be a big issue. Just because someone asks if you want life insurance doesn't mean you can get it.

8. Always be covered. The best kind of life insurance is in force when you die.

If you are dependent on someone else, it is your busi-ness to know how you are protected. Whether you are a breadwinner, homemaker or business partner, you are indispensable. So when you make financial plans for the future, think how life insurance could provide for your family if anything were to happen to you - because life insurance isn't for people who die, it is for the people who live.

INSURANCE TO BEWARE AND BE AWARE OF

Beware of:

1. The first one that comes to mind is the advertisement that guarantees you life insurance with no medicals and no salesperson. This insurance only becomes effective two years after being issued and costs twice as much as regular life insurance. The only people that this insurance is good for are those who have been declined for regular insurance.

2. Life insurance offered to you by your "Friendly Bank" Insurance Company is an expensive five-year guaranteed renewable, but not guaranteed cost type of insurance. One can purchase a fully guaranteed ten-year term (not just five year) for 4% less than the banks, with no worry of unexpected increase.

3. Mortgage Insurance offered by the banks, especially if you are nonsmokers. You can usually obtain less costly, fully transferable (from house to house), and nonreducing life insurance. Mortgage insurance

only pays off the mortgage upon the death of one partner. But what if you wanted the cash and liked the mortgage because it was at a very low rate? Sorry, not possible with the banks.

Be aware of the following:

1. Insurance companies now have a lump sum living benefit plan. This plan pays a lump sum of up to $1,000,000 if you have a heart attack, a stroke, most cancers, kidney failure, vital organ transplants, paralysis, multiple sclerosis, blindness, and deafness (e.g., initial cost for a forty-year-old male is only $527 per year for a $100,000 lump sum - tax-free). One hundred percent of the premiums paid are refunded on death if nothing was paid out. This plan can be purchased between ages eighteen and sixty-five. These illnesses are usually telling you to change your lifestyle or die. Can you afford to slow down and smell the roses? This benefit is tax-free.

2. Hospital insurance is now available. This will pay (over and above other insurance) $100 or $200 per day for every day you or one of your family are in the hospital. When diagnosed with some illnesses (like cancer, stroke, etc.), it also pays a lump sum of $2,000 to $4,000. These benefits are tax-free.

3. Annual travel insurance. If you go for man many trips per year, but all for less than fifteen days at a time, you could have outside of Canada medical

insurance for $50 or less. Sounds too good to be true, but it is available. This is great for business people and cross-border shoppers. The cost is tax deductible.

Tax Planning

Our own governments represent the greatest threat to your money. Taxes have increased 1,167% since 1961

WHAT IS TAX PLANNING?

While tax evasion is illegal and can result in severe financial penalties and punishment in the courts, tax minimization is an important element of your financial plan because of the increasing burden of taxation facing all Canadians. Every Canadian has the right to manage their financial affairs and utilize all legitimate opportunities offered by the Income Tax Act to plan and structure their financial affairs in such a way as to preserve as much of their income as possible for investment purposes.

WHAT DO THE RICH DO?

Since most Canadians have very little knowledge of tax planning strategies, this is an area in which we can all learn a great deal from "what the rich do." The first thing to remember is that for wealthy Canadians, tax planning strategies are the cornerstones of their personal financial plan. Every financial decision they make has important tax consequences which must be considered. Because most middle and upper income Canadians pay more than half of their income in taxes of various kinds, it is essential for these people to minimize the tax impact as much as possible. For this reason, many more people are now likely to include tax advantaged strategies and investments (such as special classes of mutual funds, limited partnerships, labour sponsored venture capital corporations, and other tax deferral investments) as part of their investment portfolio.

For the record, here are two concise definitions:

Tax Evasion: The illegal practice of deliberately not reporting or understating taxable income by failing to report all or a portion of income received or by claiming fictitious deductions such as on excess number of personal exemptions.

Tax Avoidance: The legitimate practice of minimizing tax liability by arranging business and financial affairs in a manner which is accepted as being within the scope of income tax law. Remember there are also special tax avoidance rules as well.

Always remember that when you are evaluating any investment that offers tax advantages, never focus exclusively on the tax benefits. Make sure the investment is attractive in its own right, even without the tax benefits. If it makes sense based on its own merits, then review the tax considerations for your particular financial situation and make your decision.

Perhaps the best advice that we can give you is to mention some of the most commonly overlooked tax deductions which many people miss when filing their personal income tax returns.

Finally, it is critically important for most people to seek professional assistance for detailed tax planning decisions. Never underestimate the value of a knowledgeable financial planner or tax accountant.

HOW TO DEFER CAPITAL GAINS

When former finance minister Michael Wilson introduced the $500,000 capital gains exemption a decade or so ago, most Canadians ignored it. After a number of years, this exemption was reduced to $100,000, and ultimately it was eliminated altogether by Paul Martin. This ended the best way Canadians had of avoiding capital gains altogether.

Currently, only 75% of capital gains are taxable at your marginal tax rate. This means an average peak rate of about 40% depending upon your province of residence. But there are still ways to defer capital gains.

Under the Income Tax Act, if you give money to children, grandchildren, nieces, or nephews under age eighteen, and the funds are invested in the minor's name in trust, the interest or dividend income earned is attributed back to you for income tax purposes.

In addition, if the funds are invested in the child's name in trust, to earn capital gains, there is no attribution and income is taxed in the child's hands. Because everyone, regardless of age has a $6,456 tax credit, the child can earn up to $10,000 a year tax free. All you have to do is file a tax return in the child's name using the child's social insurance number, reporting the gain each and every year up to the child's eighteenth birthday.

Remember, it's your money held in trust so you can take it back anytime (including the capital gains) tax free with no reporting obligations.

If the child or grandchild is eight years old, by the time they reach age eighteen, you will have sheltered over $100,000 in tax-free gains. If you have several minor children, grandchildren, nieces, or nephews, this means hundreds of thousands of tax-free gains through income splitting like this.

TAX DEFERRED MUTUAL FUNDS

A second option is permissible through the purchase of capital gains exempt shares of three well known mutual fund companies. Since 1987, fund companies could issue shares of the same fund in different classes (for example: A, B, C, D class shares, etc.). Each class of shares represents a different mutual fund group with different investment objective. As you moved back and forth between the different classes of shares you have the same adjusted cost base. Therefore, you have the same acquisition cost and no taxable capital gain as long as you hold any of the shares and don't liquidate them into cash. This is in contrast to transferring money between different funds in which capital gains are taxable at the time of each transaction. This is equivalent to a second RRSP but without the deductions. You are earning unlimited capital gains outside the RRSP which can be transferred into your estate.

THREE UNIQUE FUND COMPANIES

The three fund companies which offer this unique share class structure are C.I., AGF, and GT Global. C.I. Sector Funds has nine different classes of shares. AGF International has nine different classes, and GT Global also has eight classes of shares.

Therefore, if your goal is to accrue tax-free gains for five to ten years and create no annual tax liability until you liquidate your position, purchase funds which offer these special classes of shares instead of their regular products. The returns generated between these special funds and their regular funds are the same, so you are not sacrificing performance.

Whether you earn $5,000 or $500,000 in these special classes and hold them five years or twenty years, there is no direct capital gains tax liability until liquidation to cash. You can move back and forth between the different classes usually without any transfer fee. For the smaller funds, there may be some minimal tax for some dividends or income above gains as shares are sold or liquidated, but the tax benefit is substantial.

Can you avoid capital gains taxes? Yes, you can — easily, and anyone can do it!

DON'T OVERLOOK THESE TAX-SAVING MEASURES

Although income tax rules and "loopholes" are being constantly tightened and/or closed by governments, there are numerous tax tips available to individuals that are often overlooked. Professional advice should be sought before implementing these tips.

Child Care Expenses

A portion of tuition fees paid to private schools for your children may be tax deductible as child care expenses.

If the lower income spouse had no income, there is usually no deduction available. However, if the lower income spouse is a full-time student at a post-secondary school, child care expenses may be claimed by the higher income spouse.

Deductible child care expenses may be paid to an older child if both parents work.

Child care expense deduction: $5,000 per child under seven, and $3,000 per child aged seven to sixteen.

Medical Expenses

Medical expenses can be claimed for any twelve-month period ending during the tax year in question. For example, if major expenses are incurred near the end of the prior year and near the beginning of the current year, all of the expenses may be claimed in the current year.

The entire cost of full-time care in a nursing home may be an eligible medical expense.

Specific medical services and accommodation costs for an individual and companion may be eligible medical expenses.

A disability tax credit is available where a person has a severe and prolonged mental or physical impairment.

Medical expense threshold remains unchanged at $1,614.

Retiring allowances and severance payments can be transferred to an RRSP within sixty days following the year of receipt, subject to certain limitations.

Employee Goods and Services Tax ("GST") rebates are available to an employee who incurs GST on employment related expenses that are tax deductible.

Tax shelter deductions to be incurred during a year can be used by an individual to obtain a reduction in income tax withholdings at source, rather than waiting until filing a tax return to receive the tax savings.

1997 Credits and Limits

Remember, inflation is under 3% so credits stay at their old levels. This is a direct tax increase.

THE JERRY WHITE TOP FIFTEEN TAX STRATEGIES

1. Medical expenses are often ignored because you get credit only when they surpass 3% of your net income. Remember, though, that eyeglasses, dental care, health insurance premiums, prescription drugs, and the cost of renovations made to your home to accommodate a disability are all eligible. So it pays to save your receipts year-round and tally them at tax time. One eligible expenditure that's often overlooked is the premiums you pay for medical insurance provided by your employer. (These premiums are the only items under this deduction you're allowed to claim without a

receipt.) You can also lump the medical expenses of both spouses and all dependent children on one return, in order to boost your claim over the threshold. As well, there's some leeway in expenditure dates: You can claim medical expenses for any twelve-month period ending in the current taxation year.

2. Charitable donations made by your spouse and yourself should be combined on one return to maximize the $200 threshold for the highest credit. Alternatively, you can stockpile charitable donation receipts for up to five years (although the deduction can never exceed 20% of your net income).

3. Political contributions generate the most generous treatment by Revenue Canada. You get a 75% tax credit for the first $100 donated, and 50% on the rest.

4. Commission income can be claimed under a section of the Income Tax Act that entitles you to "salesmen's expenses" similar to the deductions available to the self-employed.

5. Single parents should remember to claim the "equivalent to married" nonrefundable credit on one of your children; it can be worth up to $1,300 in saved taxes.

6. Disability credits are often overlooked. To find out if you or a family member may be eligible (a doctor's assessment will be necessary) refer to Revenue Canada's pamphlet, "Tax information for people with disabilities."

7. Nonrefundable tax credits, such as pension and disability credits, received by one spouse can be transferred to a spouse in cases where he or she doesn't have enough income to use them.

8. Unused tuition fee credits can be transferred to a spouse, parent, or grandparent even if they don't support the student.

9. Deduct safety deposit box charges and other expenses paid to manage your investment assets. This includes RRSP trustee fees, provided they were paid with cash from outside your RRSP.

10. Provincial tax credits shouldn't be overlooked. Because you have to fill out a separate form, many people are unaware of them.

11. Claim all your child care costs. Eligible expenses include everything from a nanny to occasional babysitting. Regardless of your babysitter's age, you can claim the expense, as long as you get a receipt. And hang on to it;

while you don't have to submit receipts, they do have to be available should Revenue Canada come back for a second look.

12. If you have children in university, make sure they file their own returns, so that you can claim any tuition fees they can't. If your children do not need all their tuition fees to reduce their federal tax payable to zero, those fees may then be transferred to you.

13. If you have changed jobs or moved make the claim. Eligible expenses include the costs of the move and any travel, accommodation, temporary living expenses, and, in some cases, costs associated with selling your former residence.

14. Claim the GST rebate on any eligible employment expenses you have. These might include the capital-cost allowance on a car, gas, and repairs.

15. Remember that any of the following amounts your spouse does not need to reduce his or her federal tax to zero can be transferred to you: the age tax credit for people over 65; the pension income deduction; disability deductions; and education expenses.

INCOME SPLITTING

- Family expenses: The easiest form of spousal income splitting applies when both mates have an income gap. Each should have a separate bank account. Then the higher-taxed spouse would pay all family expenses, leaving the other's full income for investment.

    Say the lower-taxed spouse owes tax when the yearly return is due. As with family expenses, the higher-taxed one can foot that bill so the money stays invested.

- Gifts and inheritances: The same principles apply as above. Say a woman, who earns far less than her husband, receives money from her parents. She should invest that in her own name to ensure future earnings are taxed at her lower rate.

    Many people have relatives outside Canada. There is no attribution on money from a person who is not a Canadian resident (for tax purposes). Say your parents, who live overseas, send your newborn $10,000. That can be invested in his or her name. You will need an account opened "in trust" since a minor is involved.

- Spousal RRSP: This is usually a long-term strategy aimed at saving future tax by enabling a couple to balance their retirement incomes. It can also work in the short term if one spouse is planning to stop work for a few years.

- Testamentary trust: This is a trust that's created on the death of the person providing the money. Say you plan to leave a heap of cash to your spouse in the expectation that he or she will use it to support the family. The investment income would all be taxable in his or her hands. But if your will carves up the money and creates a trust for each family member, each person's share of the income can be taxed at his or her progressive rates.

- Child tax benefit: This can be invested in your child's name without attribution. It's a good way to save for post-secondary education.

- Registered education savings plans: Investment earnings are tax-deferred until withdrawn, when the earnings are taxed in the student's hands.

- Child's allowance: Your child has a part-time or summer job. The child invests all take-home pay for college while you pay an equivalent allowance for spending now.

- C/QPP splitting: Retirees can have up to half their Canada or Quebec Pension Plan payments made to their spouses if both are at least sixty. The split depends on a formula that factors in the contribution periods and marriage duration, but can be up to $4,000 a year.

- Self-employment: The self-employed can pay

spouses and children reasonable salaries for bona fide business services. Along with income splitting, this makes the recipient eligible for unemployment insurance, C/QPP, and RRSP contributions.

1997 Combined Federal-Provincial Marginal Tax Rates

Province	Dividends %	Capital gains %	Other income %
British Columbia	36.6	40.6	54.2
Alberta	31.4	34.6	46.1
Saskatchewan	36.5	39.0	52.0
Manitoba	36.3	37.8	50.4
Ontario	35.0	38.8	51.8
Quebec	38.7	39.7	52.9
New Brunswick	34.5	38.3	51.1
Nova Scotia	33.8	37.5	50.0
P.E.I.	34.0	37.7	50.3
Newfoundland	36.0	40.0	53.3
Yukon	31.4	34.9	46.6
Northwest Territories	30.0	33.3	44.4

Source: KPMG

THE NEW THREATS TO YOUR CAPITAL

As if life was not already taxing enough, the government has instituted a series of changes which may affect many of our readers.

First, the government terminated the very popular mutual fund limited partnership investment effective November 19, 1996. Second, the government is aggressively working to disallow many real estate limited partnerships and businesses established without reasonable contemplation of profit.

For example, if someone establishes a domestic yacht charter business and only creates operating losses for several years, Revenue Canada has argued that these losses should not be allowed. However, a court has ruled that the taxpayer has the right to be a bad business person or make imprudent investments that create losses as in many recent real estate deals Revenue Canada is appealing.

The most disturbing change is, however, the new Migratory Tax Law that came into effect retroactive to October 1, 1996. This law affects those who are outside of Canada for long periods of time or who wish to move to the U.S. or Caribbean and no longer remain a Canadian resident for tax purposes.

The law was introduced by the minister of finance because of the highly publicized Bronfman case of 1991, when they received an advanced ruling from the Tax Department allowing the family to move $2 billion from Canada to the United States without any taxes being paid.

Now, the government deems you to have sold your Canadian assets-stocks, bonds, business shares, etc., if you are leaving Canada to take up residency for tax purposes elsewhere. This means that under the new rules, you can't just take your money and run. You are now restricted (as in Australia and Denmark) to the proceeds from the sale of your principal residence and $25,000 without being subject to taxes. If you wish to remove more money, you must declare it all to Revenue Canada and pay capital gains tax on it prior to departure from Canada.

If your solicitor is working for you on the sale of a business or investments, they may be required to withhold 30% for remission to Revenue Canada.

This is the most onerous migration tax law in the major western economies.

If you plan to change residences or even establish a business in the U.S. and secure a green card, you may have substantial new tax liability. Consult your tax advisor before you take that extended trip.

Tax Shelters		
Common pitfall	Typical shelters	Royalty trusts
Risky	Can be risky, depending on underlying business.	Generally lower risk, although interest rate and commodity price fluctuations will have an impact.
Costly	Often cost thousands of dollars.	Trust units can be purchased on the open market for very little - much like stocks.
Cashflow	Often little or no cashflow depending on underlying business.	Generally a healthy income stream is provided; often partially or fully tax sheltered.
Alternative minimum tax	Can be a problem where large deductions are provided.	Never a problem since deductions are not claimed on personal tax return.
Offensive to Revenue Canada	More and more shelters have been closed down recently, expect this trend to continue.	Have the tax man's stamp of approval currently; no apparent reason for government to take offense.

Source: Tim Cestnick, published in The Globe and Mail, *November 30, 1996*

ULTIMATE BUSINESS - TAX PLANNING FOR THE OWNER/MANAGER

Owner/managers have some valuable tools at their disposal for building tax benefits. Here are some of our top picks.

1. You may pay a reasonable salary to a spouse or child for work performed in a family business.

2. If your company has taxable income of $200,000 or less, you should consider taking remuneration in the form of dividends rather than salary.

3. If your company has more than $200,000 of taxable income, you may consider accruing bonuses to reduce taxable income to $200,000, provided the accrued bonuses are paid within 179 days of the company's year-end.

4. If your company has realized capital gains, the untaxed portion (25%) of the gains should be paid as a tax-free dividend out of the company's capital dividend account.

5. To maximize your 1996 RRSP contribution, salary or other earned income must be at least $75,000 in 1995.

6. You can deduct 50% of the business-related expenses for food and beverages and tickets for the theatre, concerts, and athletic events.

7. If you are a shareholder in your company and you borrow money or otherwise become indebted to the corporation, you must repay the debts by the end of the fiscal period following the fiscal period in which the indebtedness arose to avoid having to include the debts in income.

8. You may require and use fixed assets, which you would normally acquire early in the following year, at the end of the current year to take early advantage of capital cost allowance (CCA).

9. If your business is losing money, you may choose not to claim certain optional deductions such as CCA.

10. If you have a partner in your business, you should enter into a shareholder's agreement to govern your current and future relationship.

INVESTMENT PLANNING - WHY A FLAT TAX - SINGLE TAX WOULD WORK

Anyone who is Mormon or Seventh-Day Adventist knows about tithing, paying 5% or 10% of your income (essentially a flat tax) to the church. The Catholic church used this concept for over 900 years.

The idea of an income tax was introduced in 1917 as a temporary measure to finance the First World War. Today, the Income Tax Act is 2,500 pages of chaos and confusion. It costs $3 billion a year to collect the taxes, and it has stimulated an underground economy estimated to be somewhere between $20 billion to $100 billion - nobody really knows. Add on the GST and Canadian taxes have increased 1,167% since 1961, and now in 1996 the average Canadian family pays total federal, provincial, and municipal taxes totalling 46.5% of income.

Are we in need of tax reform? You bet! Canada has always maintained a graduated or progressive tax system. The idea was always to make the successful, rich, and achievers pay more as a percentage of total income. In fact, the Organization for Economic Cooperation and Development identifies Canada's tax system as the least equitable and most unfair to high-income earners.

Since the early 1960s, there has been much debate about changing to a flat tax system with a single tax rate. Professor Milton Friedman and over half a dozen Nobel laureates in economics have all written in favour of a flat tax system.

In Canada, the federal government has established a committee led by the deputy minister of finance, Donald Dodge, to review our tax system. Both the Reform Party and Jean Charest of the Conservatives will be advocating a flat tax approach in the next federal election.

In the United States, the flat tax has been the subject of much debate in the Republican primaries led by Steve Forbes and Jack Kemp.

The single tax system is not the idea of a bunch of "nutty" individuals like the Flat Earth Society. It is a well-conceived concept in place in many Asian countries, including Hong Kong, with very positive implications and results.

The impact on Canada of a single tax system with a 20% federal tax rate is clear. Costs of tax collection would probably fall from $3 billion to $300 million. The underground economy and black market would be sharply reduced adding to total government income. Entrepreneurs would be faced with less paperwork and lower taxes. Tax lawyers and accountants currently fighting 37,000 cases before the courts would have to spend their days doing something else.

The tax return would be a single page with credits only for RRSPs, age, and charities. Tax shelters would no longer be needed or available. For corporations, a credit for value added and capital cost allowance would keep their filings simple.

Corporations would no longer reserve the billions in tax credits, subsidies, and tax incentives hidden in the Income Tax Act.

With provincial taxes at 50% of the federal rate, the average rate would be a total of 30%. All income would be treated the same and the 1,100,000 entrepreneurs in this country who create the jobs would be singularly better off as would the overwhelming majority of tax-payers who would end up paying less.

The flat tax or single tax system is not some passing new political idea. It is the type of reform that makes immense sense for Canada.

CONCLUSION

This book is meant to illustrate the financial and investment habits of Canada's top 1% of income earners. The strategies and habits have validity for us all. It is not age, income, education, or sex that determines financial success. It is personality. People who are positive, assertive, confident, and action-oriented succeed. Those who are negative, pessimistic, and afraid to make decisions do not. This is a lesson for all Canadians. Act on it and make money! Learn to do what the rich do.

Appendix

Financial Wisdom At a Glance

These are important charts and tables to help you make more informed decisions.

Ranking of goals and objectives

Goals	Priority				Time Limit			
	most important	very important	important	least important	1 year	2-4 years	5 years or more	$ to attain goals
Change job								
Continue education								
Raise a family								
Own a home								
Increase payments on mortgage								
Supplement income								
Provide for children's education								
Buy a cottage								
Provide for future expenses								
Make preretirement plans								
Maintain lifestyle at retirement								
Increase savings for a rainy day								
Decrease debts								
Review insurance coverages								

Types of Diversification

"Is diversification the "strategy of ignorance" or does it really reduce riek?"

Company Diversification
Buying many different equities. Experience shows that at fifteen stocks, we eliminate most of the systematic risks of the markets.

Industry Diversification
All industries have cycles when they are in and out of favour because of changing economic and business conditions. Therefore, we need to diversify by industry to mitigate risk.

Geographic Diversification
This does not just mean investing across Canada or the U.S. It means investing globally. Although markets are getting more closely aligned, the alignment is not perfect, and we can reduce risks by investing in markets that are more independent and less affected by North American trends.

Diversified Companies
When we meet blue chip stocks or high-end equity mutual funds, we should read the prospectus to determine the size and status of the companies in the fund. The larger and more diversified the companies, the lower the probability of a major downturn or collapse.

Cluster Investing
A little known concept developed in 1991 which indicates that although you might purchase eight to fifteen stocks or eight different mutual funds, you might still be too heavily located in one or two investment clusters such as growth stocks or government bonds. The concept presents five low-risk clusters: basic industries, growth, oil, utilities, and consumers/cyclical. A portfolio from each of the five should aid in reducing risk and stabilizing the portfolio over time.

The Investment Risk Hierarchy

1. High Risk
- Commodities
- Futures
- Options
- High-Risk Bonds (Junk)
- Gold and Precious Metals
- Sector Mutual Funds

2. High-Moderate Risk
- Investment Quality Corporate Bonds
- Blue Chip Stocks
- Speculative Small Company Growth Stocks
- Real Estate Limited Partnership

3. Moderate Risk
- Precious Metal Mutual Funds
- International Equity and Bond Mutual Funds
- Domestic Growth Equity Mutual Funds
- Balanced Mutual Funds
- Bond Funds

4. High-Low Range
- Government of Canada Bonds
- Money Market Mutual Funds

5. Low Range
- T-Bills
- Bank Deposits — Insured

Investor types

Type	%	Attitude & Philosophy
The Risktaker	13	Need risk to succeed at anything
The Conservative	19	Safety, security, responsibility
The Provider	16	Altruistic, sharing
The Spendthrift	14	Live well and die
The Acquisitor	13	Controlled by money
The Indifferent	15	Need just enough to get by
The Idealist	10	Not emotionally concerned about money

Portfolio Performance Determinants

Other factors	Market timing	Security selection	Asset allocation policy
1%	2%	6%	91%

Types of Mutual Funds

Fund Type	Portfolio Mix	Investment Objective	Risk Factor
Money Market Funds	Short-term government bonds, T-Bills, blue chips corporate debt securities	Regular income from interest and safety of principal	Low

205

Mortgage Funds	Residential and commercial mortgages	Interest income	Low
Fixed Income Funds	Government bonds, blue chip corporate bonds, debentures, mortgages, preferred shares	Moderate income from interest and dividends	Moderate
Balanced Funds	Preferred shares, short- and medium-term bonds, and blue chip common shares	Income from dividends and interest, some capital gain potential	Moderate — varies according to overall mix
Dividend Income Funds	Preferred shares, blue chip common shares	High dividend income, some capital gain, dividend tax credits	Moderate
Growth Funds	Common shares with growth potential	High capital gain potential	High — market trends are accentuated
International Funds	Common shares, bonds outside of Canada	Dividend income, interest, and capital gains	Moderate to high — varies according to overall mix

How Wealthy Canadians are Different

Wealthy Canadians
77% possess a self-directed RRSP
87% contribute to an RRSP every year
62% contribute the maximum allowable amount into their RRSP every year
68% state that despite Canada's financial problems, they plan to retire in Canada

National averages in 1996
34% of all Canadians made an RRSP contribution — average contribution $4,000

24% of all female tax filers made an RRSP contribution
15% of all tax filers under the age of thirty made an RRSP contribution
The average annual contribution was $950
Average holdings in RRSP — $31,000

The Benefits of Contributing to an RRSP

— future value of a $1,000 investment in a GIC after tax

Years	6%	8%	10%	12%	14%	16%
1	1,028	1,038	1,047	1,056	1,066	1,075
5	1,149	1,203	1,258	1,316	1,375	1,437
10	1,321	1,445	1,583	1,731	1,891	2,065
15	1,518	1,740	1,992	2,277	2,601	2,967
20	1,744	2,092	2,506	2,996	3,577	4,264
25	2,004	2,516	3,153	3,942	4,919	6,127
30	2,303	3,026	3,966	5,186	6,765	8,804
35	2,647	3,640	4,990	6,823	9,304	12,651

— future value of a $1,000 investment in RRSPs

Years	6%	8%	10%	12%	14%	16%
1	1,060	1,080	1,100	1,120	1,140	1,160
5	1,338	1,469	1,611	1,762	1,925	2,100
10	1,791	2,159	2,594	3,016	3,707	4,411
15	2,397	3,172	4,177	5,474	7,138	9,266
20	3,207	4,661	6,727	9,646	13,743	19,461
25	4,292	6,848	10,835	17,000	26,462	40,874
30	5,743	10,063	17,449	29,960	50,950	85,850
35	7,686	14,785	28,102	52,800	98,100	180,314

Wealthy Canadians' Ten Most Common Tax Planning Options

Income Splitting
Particularly if you have self-employed earnings, it is smart to have another family member receive income instead of yourself if this other family member is subject to taxation at a lower level.

Spousal RRSP
Consider putting money into an RRSP in the name of your spouse. If

your spouse is in a lower tax bracket, on their retirement, your spouse will be able to take out income at a lower tax rate.

Tax Deferral Opportunities

The most obvious, and important, of these is your RRSP which allows your contributions to accumulate over many years tax free. At age 71, your RRSP funds can then be transferred into a Registered Retirement Income Fund (RRIF) to further defer tax.

Tax Shelters

Products such as Limited Partnerships and Labour Sponsored Venture Capital Corporations can save on taxes for qualified investors as well as present opportunities for capital appreciation if they are also quality investments.

Non-Taxable Benefits

Try to structure any compensation you may receive to take maximum advantage of tax benefits. For example, the $25,000 in life insurance that your employer may offer you that is not taxable.

Tax Deductible Debt

Interest expense incurred for the purpose of earning income, whether investment income or business income, is deductible. However, interest expense incurred from credit cards or a home mortgage is not deductible and therefore offers no tax advantage.

RRSP

Contribute annually to an RRSP, especially a self-directed RRSP, if possible.

Dividends

Dividends are beneficial because they are subject to the dividend tax credit. Convert highly taxable interest income into lower taxed dividend income.

Capital Gains

Alter your investment strategy by refocussing away from non-deductible interest income into capital gains investment opportunities.

Withholding Tax

Use any opportunity to reduce the amount of withholding tax at source which will allow you greater flexibility in your tax planning and may increase the income you have for investment purposes.